Liz Earle

ILLUSTRATED
NATURAL
BEAUTY

For Paddy
Facile princeps

ACKNOWLEDGMENTS

I should like to thank all those who shared their valuable knowledge with me whilst researching and writing this book. In particular, I am grateful to Len and Shirley Price, Pat Suthers, Jan Kusmerick of Fragrant Earth and also to Geraldine Howard of Aromatherapy Associates for their aromatherapy expertise and valuable information on essential oils. I must also thank my saintly mother, who twice-tested every natural beauty recipe, Andrew Harrison MRPharmS for his technical advice, and my talented researchers Sarah Hamilton-Fleming and Karen Swan-MacLeod for their additional in-put. My gratitude also to Iain Philpott for his cover photography, hairdresser Terence Renati and make-up artist Vicki Partridge.

Note

This book is a reference guide. The suggestions given are not intended to be a substitute for medical advice or treatment. Any application of the ideas or recommendations in this book is at the reader's own discretion.

Liz Earle

ILLUSTRATED
NATURAL
BEAUTY

CRESCENT
BOOKS

New York • Avenel

This edition is published by Crescent Books,
distributed by Random House Value Publishing, Inc.,
40 Engelhard Avenue, Avenel, New Jersey 07001.

Random House
New York . Toronto . London . Sydney . Auckland

Project Editors: Veronica Sperling and Christine McFadden
Design and typesetting: Sara Kidd
Photographer: Marie-Louise Avery
Home Economist: Emma-Lee Gow
Stylist: Kay McGlone
Botanical photographs: Karl Adamson

ISBN 0-517-18459-1

Printed and bound in Singapore by Tien Wah Press

A CIP catalog record for this book is available from the Library of Congress.

8 7 6 5 4 3 2 1

CONTENTS

INTRODUCTION

We all use some sort of skincare – be it a swift scrub with soap and water or some of the more sophisticated age-defying day creams. Modern cosmetology is shrouded in technical mystery and yet the formulae for many of our health and beauty remedies today are based on traditional techniques that have been handed down over the generations. In fact, modern scientific research is now endorsing much of the folklore surrounding natural therapies that have been used for centuries.

Making your own health and beauty preparations is fun and easy to follow. It can also save a great deal of money. Water and alcohol are the two most commonly used skincare ingredients, so why pay pounds for a product that contains only a few pence worth of ingredients? Unless you choose products that contain genuinely high levels of natural ingredients, you may be better off with homemade remedies. These can contain much more useful amounts of active ingredients such as essential fatty acids, vitamins and enzymes. In addition, you may tailor many lotions and potions to suit your own individual needs and make many remedies for yourself, your family and friends.

The recipes in this book range from simple blends of massage oils to more detailed descriptions of making soap and skin cream, for the more adventurous. Effective treatments for skin problems such as acne, eczema, psoriasis and ageing skin are also included. You will find practical background information on all the ingredients used and where you can obtain them. Unlike many shop-bought toiletries, your own products avoid animal testing and you can choose to buy cruelty-free ingredients. You can also re-cycle containers and cut down on the enormous amount of packaging waste produced by commercial manufacturers.

With the help of this book you will be able to transform your kitchen into a beauty playground and fill your bathroom shelves with therapeutic treatments for your face, hair and entire body.

NATURAL BEAUTY
IN HISTORY

Natural beauty care has played an important part in history, since the earliest civilisations when mankind first used many of the plants and other elements provided by nature. The pioneers of natural beauty treatments were probably the cave people living in the Mesolithic period around 10,000 BC, who applied grease and castor oil to soften the skin, and tattooed their bodies with plant dyes as protection from the sun. Recorded formulae for skin softening lotions date back to Biblical times, where women made lotions from olive oil and spices which were often rubbed into sore feet to keep them smooth and supple. Scented barks and dried roots were finely ground to make talcum powders and precious aromatic oils were often rubbed into the hair to keep it smelling sweet.

EGYPTIAN LIPS

The first lipsticks were made in the ancient city of Ur, near Babylon, some 5000 years ago. Next door in Egypt, Cleopatra relied on several hundreds of natural beauty remedies to maintain her legendary powers of seduction. Her fragrances may have literally changed the face of history as Mark Antony was intoxicated by the scent of rose and patchouli oils on her skin. Cleopatra's beauty routine included bathing in ass's milk and applying face packs made from crushed sesame seeds and barley. Like most Egyptian women, she also favoured the use of henna and walnut oil to keep her hair dark and glossy, and used black kohl crayons made from powdered antimony (a type of metal) around her eyes to dramatic effect. Her shimmering blue and green eyeshadows were made from finely ground semi-precious stones such as lapis lazuli and malachite, which had a practical as well as cosmetic purpose as they shielded the skin from the sun's strong rays. Less appealing were Cleopatra's

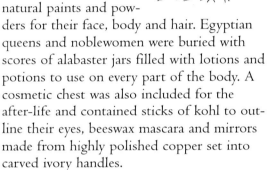

lipsticks and rouge which came from the deep red pigment of finely crushed carmine beetles and powdered ant's eggs.

The women of Thebes and those who lived alongside the Nile were reputed to be the most beautiful in the world and they certainly made full use of the many natural paints and powders for their face, body and hair. Egyptian queens and noblewomen were buried with scores of alabaster jars filled with lotions and potions to use on every part of the body. A cosmetic chest was also included for the after-life and contained sticks of kohl to outline their eyes, beeswax mascara and mirrors made from highly polished copper set into carved ivory handles.

Compared to other cultures of that time, the Egyptians were extremely vain and prided themselves on their appearance. It is no coincidence that cosmetics were first developed by the Ancient Egyptians and drawings depicting the extensive use of elaborate eye make-up have been found in tombs built as far back as 5000 BC. Surprisingly, remains of eye make-up found in the pyramids show that it was often made from fairly harsh substances, such as lead sulphide and charcoal which would have irritated their eyes. Reddish brown face paints contained clays with a high iron content to give them their colour, and there was even an anti-wrinkle remedy made from bullock's bile and ostrich eggs! Fortunately, these natural remedies have not stood the test of time, although many other Egyptian innovations remain relevant.

ORIGINAL SKIN

The Ancient Egyptians can probably take the credit for devising most of the earliest beauty preparations and they were especially fond of highly aromatic perfumes. Relics found in the pyramids include precious perfume flasks and essential oil carriers, placed there to keep their owners smelling sweet in the after-life. Aromatic oils were sold by Arab traders who travelled across the Middle East with precious cargoes of spices, frankincense and myrrh strapped to their camels. These were highly prized and were worth even more than gold. We can learn a great deal of useful information from the beauty recipes that have been handed down from years gone by.

In addition to cosmetics and perfumes, the Ancient Egyptians were the first to develop soap, made from a natural cleanser called saponin, which is extracted from the soaproot or soapwort plant. They also added animal fats and fragrant oils to the soap formula and used them for household cleaning as well as bathing. The Assyrians in the Middle East added precious perfumed oils too, to their washing water and were scrupulous about personal hygiene. Body-smoothing products were popular and skin scrubs first made their appearance around 1000 BC. These were made from powdered pumice stone and used by Assyrian women to buff the body and keep the skin smooth. Before showering (which they did frequently), the Egyptians and Assyrians would rub themselves with handfuls of sand to clean the pores.

BRAIDS AND BEARDS

Both the Assyrian men and women took great pride in their hair and it was always worn elaborately braided, oiled and perfumed. Tiny balls of perfumed wax were tucked close to the scalp so that during long banquets the fragrance would be released by body heat and trickle down the neck to last throughout the evening. Men kept their beards trimmed like topiary into exotic shapes, and facial hair was such an important symbol of strength and power that several Egyptian queens took to wearing a false gilded beard on ceremonial occasions.

Applying make-up for a night out obviously took a great deal of time, as is illustrated by the cosmetic box of Thuthu, the wife of a nobleman, kept in the British Museum. It contains the following necessities: sandals, elbow pads (for resting on, as putting on make-up was a lengthy process), pumice stones to smooth the skin and remove body hair, eye pencils of wood and ivory to apply powdered colour, a bronze dish for mixing colours and three pots of face cream.

The Ancient Greeks also knew a thing or two about cosmetics, although their mascara made from a mixture of gum and soot does seem a bit crude. Greek women painted their cheeks with herbal pastes made from crushed berries and seeds to give them a healthy looking glow. They also developed a more dangerous habit of using white lead and mercury on their faces, to give the complexion a chalky appearance. Unbeknown to them, these heavy metals were absorbed through the skin and resulted in many untimely deaths — an unfortunate trend which continued down the ages.

The Greek physician Galen recognised the problem and wrote, 'women who often paint themselves with mercury, though they be very young, they presently turn old and withered and have wrinkled faces like an ape'. As well as being a first-class physician, Galen is also credited with the original recipe for cold cream, based on beeswax, olive oil and rosewater. He also remarked that garden snails, when finely ground, made an effective moisturiser and the unfortunate creatures were used in beauty preparations for several centuries. Less unpleasant Greek customs included using natural henna to stain finger and toe-nails red in much the same way as we paint ours with polish today. They also made false eyebrows from dyed goat's hair, which they attached to the skin with natural gums and resins.

It was the Romans, however, who established many of our modern beauty habits. As the Roman Empire swept through Europe it left behind a legacy of daily bathing in communal baths scented with rosewater.

The Romans also introduced the habit of regular shaving for men, with razors made from sharpened bronze. Rich noblemen and women continued to bathe in ass's milk and Nero's Queen Poppeia travelled with her own string of donkeys to provide the milk for her baths. Roman noblewomen also popularised the use of natural cosmetics in Britain by wearing kohl around their eyes, painting their cheeks with red paste made from beetle shells and rubbing sweet-smelling aromatic oils into their hair.

One aspect of their appearance which took up a great deal of time, was the dyeing and dressing of their hair. The Romans used many different types of natural hair dyes, including one made from the mineral quick-lime, which gave their hair a lustrous, reddish-gold tinge. Walnut oil made by steeping walnut shells in olive oil was also used to keep the hair dark brown when it began to turn grey. In Ancient Rome, blonde hair was initially considered to be a symbol of a prostitute, but with the arrival of the Scandinavian slave girls, noblewomen began to dye their own naturally dark hair lighter shades of blonde using a concentrated infusion of saffron flowers. Rosemary and juniper were the main ingredients in hair tonics reputed to prevent hair loss, and emollient skin soothers were made from saffron flowers and beeswax.

Pliny the Elder also records the use of many natural beauty ingredients, including quince cream from Cos, saffron from Rhodes and rosewater from Phaselis. He also notes the extensive use of *chypre* from Cyprus, a musky, long-lasting perfume. Many of these ingredients are still present in modern cosmetics and can be used in several effective homemade remedies. Other natural ingredients that have fortunately not stood the test of time quite so well include crocodile dung which, believe it or not, was a popular Roman face pack.

BEAUTY IN BRITAIN
When the Romans invaded Britain they were appalled to find that the native inhabitants did not believe in bathing and quickly set about building communal baths, some of which still exist in spa towns such as Bath (hence its name). However, once they had departed Britain during the fourth century, the practice of regular bathing died out, except for the occasional cold water plunge undertaken as a penance. Despite this lack of routine cleanliness, women during the Middle Ages did continue to wear some form of make-up, although rouge was only worn by shady ladies of the night.

Noblewomen continued to use white lead on their faces; they plucked their eyebrows and stained their lips dark red with plant dyes.

Natural skincare remedies were also popular and most noblewomen had their own favourite recipes for keeping the complexion smooth. To combat the destructive effects of wearing lead paste on the face, masks were made using ground asparagus roots and goat's milk, which were rubbed into the skin with pieces of warm bread. Elaborate braided hair styles were also popular and a kind of hair gel was made from a mixture of swallow droppings and lizard tallow.

During the Crusades, knights returned home with all kinds of exotic preparations never before seen in Britain. Essential oils became popular as perfumes and were also used as antiseptics to ward off the plague. The technique of soap-making was also imported from Italy, although for centuries to come soap was mainly used for washing dishes and clothes, not bodies.

THE RENAISSANCE

The next era to literally change the face of history was the Renaissance, a period of great learning and cultural development which saw many improvements in the world of natural beauty. Ladies in Venice, including Catherine de Medici, even established their own society for cosmetic testing and beauty training. However, their new-found knowledge did not stop them from continuing to use the destructive lead paint on their faces, neck and cleavage. One new invention was the beauty spot, originally made from small circles of black velvet, used to hide blemishes, such as warts, pimples and pox scars.

The philosophy of personal hygiene was also gaining ground and the first commercial toothpowders appeared, usually made from a mixture of dried sage, nettles and powdered clay. In the 1500s, Venetian noblewomen would also dye their hair by applying lotions derived from saffron flowers or sulphur and baking them on to their heads by sitting in the hot summer sun.

Although the Europeans in general were still suspicious of regular bathing (they believed that it weakened the body) they used a great deal of perfume, presumably to mask the inevitably unpleasant smell of body odour. In 1508 one of the first European perfumeries was set up by monks of the Dominican Brotherhood in Florence. They produced many popular fragrances included rhubarb elixir and melissa water, and developed scented orris powder made from ground iris roots, which were used to perfume clothes and household linen.

A FRAGRANT REIGN

Queen Elizabeth I imported many Italian and French fragrances, including scented kid gloves which were made in the hillside village of Grasse in the south of France. Life in Grasse originally revolved around the tannery industry, but perfume quickly became more popular then gloves and other leather goods, so the village turned into one of the leading fragrance centres in the world. Queen Elizabeth I was also one of Britain's most celebrated users of natural beauty preparations and her many portraits illustrate her passion for red wigs and painted skin.

Meanwhile, Elizabethan ladies still used white lead face paint and toxic mercury sulphide for rouge. Horace Walpole later wrote of 'that pretty young woman, Lady Fortrose . . . at point of death, killed like Lady Coventry and others of white lead, of which nothing could break her.' Lady Coventry herself was only twenty-seven when she died from lead poisoning absorbed through her skin. The poisonous white lead was mixed with vinegar to form a paste called ceruse. The finest was thought to come from Venice and was very expensive. The less wealthy fared much better as they had to use cheaper, safer alternatives made from sulphur and borax. White lead made the hair fall out and the extensive use of ceruse throughout the Elizabethan era explains the fashion for high foreheads, as hairlines were eroded.

Another reason for hair loss was the use of the corrosive oil of vitriol (sulphuric acid) mixed with rhubarb juice as a hair tonic and lightener. Lipsticks were a somewhat safer blend of cochineal and beeswax, and finely ground mother-of-pearl became popular as an iridescent eyeshadow. Although bathing was not fashionable, the ladies of the court did take care to keep their complexions clean. The great Queen herself washed her face alternately in red wine and ass's milk, while others used rainwater or even their urine.

Herbal infusions were also used to keep the skin clear, including fennel and eyebright water. On the rare occasions when their hair was cleaned, it was not washed but dry shampooed using finely powdered clays that were combed through to absorb the build-up of grease and dirt. Whisked egg whites were used to tighten and glaze the skin, and beauty spots remained a popular ploy for concealing blemishes. Freckles were frowned upon and one remedy for their removal calls for an infusion of elder leaves mixed with birch sap and brimstone (sulphur) to be applied to the skin by moonlight and removed in the morning with fresh butter. Bear's grease was a popular base for rouge and skin creams, and make-up pencils were made by mixing plaster of Paris with plant pigments to form sticks, which were dried in the sun.

During the reign of Charles I, the first British toiletry company set up shop in London. A young Mr Yardley is recorded as paying the monarch a large sum to gain the concession to manufacture soap for the whole of the capital. Unfortunately, the records of his activities were destroyed in the Great Fire of London, in 1666, but we do know that Yardley used lavender as the main perfume ingredient. From this time on, skincare remedies became increasingly refined and ladies of the court of James II used moisturisers made from spices and vanilla pods infused in honey. However, the use of lead-based ceruse on the complexions continued, so the trend for high foreheads and an absence of eyebrows was still fashionable. Children had their brows covered in walnut oil to decrease hair growth and eyebrows were shaved and replaced with more delicate versions made from mouse skin. Balls of fine shaving soap also appeared for the men, who would have visited a cut-throat barber for their daily shave.

In 1786 an Act of Parliament was passed to tax cosmetics, and from this we can derive an accurate list of what was available at the time. The cosmetics listed include essences, powders, wash balls and pomades such as 'tincture of peach kernels', 'essence of bouquet' and 'carnation of lilies'. Make-up pigments included rouge, blanche, vegetable rouge (made from the safflower thistle) and serviette rouge (applied to the cheeks with a small cloth). There was also 'liquid bloom of roses', 'cold cream' and 'beautifying cream'.

THE WIG REVOLUTION
By the time of the French Revolution in 1789, natural cosmetics for both men and women of the Court were the height of fashion. Elaborate powdered wigs, rouge and face powder were used extensively, with the men often wearing far more than the women.

Although shampoo had by now been invented, it was common for courtiers to keep their natural hair short and unwashed while wearing a wig on top. These were often so large that several unfortunate noblewomen died from burns suffered when their head-pieces brushed passed the candlelit chandeliers. As the wigs were made from a mass of wool and animal grease they were highly combustible and a huge fire risk. The wigs were extremely expensive and children were employed to sit on an adult's shoulders and snatch them from the heads of courtiers as they rode past in their open carriages.

From this time onwards it became fashionable to appear pale and interesting, and women's fashions focused on flimsy muslin dresses which were both diaphanous and daring. Sometimes they were even dampened to make them cling, often resulting in bronchitis and pneumonia for the unfortunate wearer. However, as the Empress Josephine had an olive complexion (she was brought up in the West Indies), she continued to make herbal rouge an essential fashion accessory.

One of the first beauty boutiques to supply the Parisian courtiers was opened in 1828 by Pierre Guerlain, founder of the famous French fragrance house. His shop was on the ground floor of the Hotel Maurice, in the Rue de Rivoli, where the dining room stands today. The many fragrant blends he created for the French Court included such patriotic perfumes as Bouquet Napoleon, Parfum de France and Eau Imperial (which is still available today). French noblewomen have a tradition of setting beauty trends and Empress Eugenie, the beautiful wife of Napoleon III, was among the first to wear and popularise mascara made from waxes and natural plant pigments.

HERBS AND HERBALISM
Over the centuries, herbalism and the study of plants had developed into an important

medical science. One of the first to document the medicinal and beautifying properties of herbs was Master-Surgeon John Gerard, who was an enthusiastic botanist as well as a respected physician.

One of his great medical advances was to identify the herb called scurvy-grass *Cochlearia officinalis,* which is rich in vitamin C and an effective cure for scurvy.

According to Gerard, the plant grew alongside the banks of the river Thames and along stretches of southern coastline – the very places where it was needed by the thousands of sailors who died from vitamin C deficiency.

In 1590, Gerard wrote a guide to herbalism which became a household bible throughout the country. Just like a well-thumbed cookery book today, Gerard's work was referred to almost daily for homemade herbal health and beauty recipes.

Probably the best-known English herbalist was Nicholas Culpeper. Born in 1616 the son of a Surrey rector, Culpeper studied Latin and medicine at Cambridge and might have gone on to become a doctor had his personal life not gone awry. After falling in love with a local girl, he borrowed £200 from his mother and ran away to get married. Culpeper arranged to meet his fiancée in Lewes, Sussex, but on the way there she was struck by lightning in a freak accident and killed. The distraught Culpeper abandoned his studies until eventually his grandfather set him up as an apprentice in a busy

London apothecary's practice. After his training, he turned his back on the lucrative medical world and opened a small shop in the deprived area of Spitalfields. Instead of prescribing expensive medicines he made 'cheap but wholesome medicines . . . not sending them to the East Indies for drugs, when they may fetch better out of their own gardens'.

Culpeper believed that common herbs could be used to great effect in medicine and revived many of the teachings of the Ancient Greek physicians such as Hippocrates and Galen. One of his favourite Biblical quotes was from Ecclesiastes: 'The Lord hath created Medicines out of the earth; and he that is wise will not abhor them'.

In 1649, Culpeper translated the *London Pharmacopoeia* into English from its original Latin – a move that outraged many doctors who preferred to keep their art secret. He went on to write his hugely popular book, *Culpeper's Complete Herbal*, which was first published in the 1600s and has been reprinted throughout the centuries until the latest edition in 1979. The book included many skincare remedies, such as an infusion of vervain and broom stalks to cleanse the skin, oatmeal boiled with vinegar to treat spots and pimples, and wheat bread soaked in rosewater to soothe tired eyes. He also recommended woodbine ointment for sunburn, thistle juice for hair loss and rosemary oil for spots.

One of the most popular books was *The Art of Beauty*, written in 1825 by an anonymous author who was quite likely to have been a doctor. Advice for ladies included erasing wrinkles by becoming overweight, applying powdered mint to reduce a large bosom and using belladonna juice from the deadly nightshade plant to enlarge the pupils of the eyes. The author also advises us not to put stays on children and to avoid tight corsets when pregnant.

A RIGID REGIME

But the doctrine for 'beauty training' makes modern health farms look like a holiday camp. Regency ladies were advised to observe the following regime:

- **Rise at six a.m.** (or five a.m. but not sooner). Briskly walk two to three miles examining the flora, fauna and clouds as you go. On returning home, change if you have perspired and dry your feet. Have all your skin, particularly that of the stomach, well rubbed with a cloth or flesh brush. Wash hands and face in cold water.
- **Breakfast** Plain biscuit (not bread), broiled underdone beefsteak or mutton chop with no fat, and half a pint mild ale.
- **Morning occupation** Out of doors, walk, garden, romp etc.
- **Dinner at two p.m.** As breakfast (no vegetables, boiled meat, fruit, sweets or pastry) plus the occasional mealy potato or boiled rice.
- **Afternoon occupation** Out of doors, walk, garden, romp etc.
- **Supper at seven p.m.** Much as breakfast and dinner.
- **Evening** At least an hour's active exercise.
- **Bedtime** Ten p.m. or earlier. Bathe feet in tepid water and rub as before.

The only advantages of this Spartan routine were to put colour back into the cheeks and to acknowledge the need to wash.

BRIGHTON BATHING

A fellow advocate of regular bathing at this time was the Prince Regent, later George IV, who installed an extensive bathroom at his Brighton Pavilion. Exclusively for men, the large tub was filled with a mixture of hot water and milk with herbs such as flax seeds (linseeds) to soften the skin. With the arrival of Queen Victoria on the throne came a new fervour for bathing throughout the country. However, there were no skin creams or cosmetics in polite society and only a dab of eau de cologne was deemed respectable. When out of doors, complexions were always protected by green veils (white netting reflected the sun and encouraged its rays) and by wearing bonnets with big brims. Inside, the face was shielded from the glare of the fire by decorated pole screens.

A CLEAN SWEEP

While the Victorians thoroughly disapproved of vanity they viewed cleanliness as being next to godliness. Soap became more widely available for those who could afford to buy it, although it was not until the middle of the century that most houses were built with indoor bathrooms. Until then, baths were taken in a tin tub in front of the sitting-room fire. At this time, soap was readily available but was sold in long anonymous bars sliced on the grocer's counter.

The first commercial soap was produced in 1884 by a Lancashire grocer called William Hesketh Lever. He had the brainwave of pre-cutting manufactured bars of soap, and stamping them with the brand name Sunlight. Demand soon overtook production and in 1888 William Lever bought a stretch of Mersey marshland and put Port Sunlight on the map of Britain. Although it sounds obvious today, William Lever's idea to give a bar of household soap a memorable name, package it properly and sell it energetically

was an entirely new marketing concept.

From these humble beginnings rose many other well-known soap brands, such as Lux, Lifebuoy and Shield – and so the mighty multinational detergent giant Lever Brothers was born. Even today, this company remains the largest supplier of soaps in the world.

Queen Victoria herself may have disapproved, but many other toiletry companies were founded during the Victorian era, including Coty and Cyclax. Yardley continued to go from strength to strength and had branched out from cakes of lavender soap into a skincare range that included Milady Powders, Lavender Vanishing Cream and Lavender Cold Cream.

Ideas for marketing and advertising began to emerge and Yardley adopted as its trademark an illustration of a group of flower sellers, with the girls holding primroses and not bunches of lavender.

At the end of the Victorian era a more relaxed attitude was taken to make-up and publications such as *Vogue* and *Queen* (now *Harpers & Queen*) magazine started to support the infant cosmetic industry. Sarah Bernhardt was reported to add half a pound of marshmallow flowers and four pounds of bran to her baths each day. She also endorsed Bernhardt Wrinkle Eradicator, a cream made from aluminium, almond milk and rosewater.

Across the Channel, Helena Rubinstein had left her native Poland and opened a salon in Paris where she sold a moisturiser called Crème Valaze. Helena was the eldest of eight sisters renowned for their beautiful complexions, and her skin cream — made by a pair of Polish chemists — became the cornerstone of what would later become her cosmetic empire.

Another Parisian contemporary of Helena Rubinstein was François Coty, a perfumier who was struggling to get his fragrances accepted in Paris. His big break came, quite literally, in 1903 when he unsuccessfully tried to get one of the larger shops to stock his scent. The manager refused even to open the bottle, but on the way out Coty smashed the bottle on the floor, the customers liked what they smelt and he was in business.

America was also busy building its own cosmetic empires and one of the first was established by Charles Meyer in 1860. A German wigmaker, Mr Meyer set up a small shop on Broadway selling Leichner's theatrical make-up, the first grease paint make in the USA. But a grease-based make-up requires something to remove it with, and for this, Pond's Extract was used – first distributed in 1846 by Theron T. Pond and later to become famous as Pond's Cold Cream.

At the turn of the century it was also discovered that zinc oxide made a good face powder which did not discolour or harm the skin, and in Hollywood, yet another immigrant wigmaker called Max Factor was making a name for himself designing make-up for the stars of the silent screen. Early movie-making was extremely primitive and stars

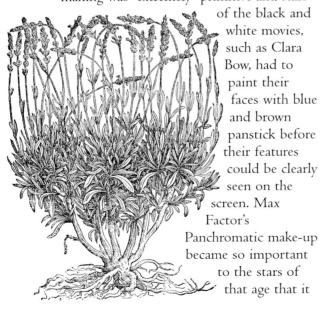

of the black and white movies, such as Clara Bow, had to paint their faces with blue and brown panstick before their features could be clearly seen on the screen. Max Factor's Panchromatic make-up became so important to the stars of that age that it

even won him an Academy Award in 1928.

As movie-making progressed, Max Factor discovered a demand for coloured pansticks and foundations for the colour 'talkies' and went on to invent a flesh-tinted make-up stick called 'Erase', which sold over 10 million units in its first year. His competitors included Elizabeth Arden, who had developed a range of make-up and skincare products based on natural ingredients. Elizabeth Arden herself was born in Canada and christened Florence Nightingale Graham – her name initially leading her to train as a nurse. However, she was so impressed by the well-groomed American women she came across that she retrained in a beauty salon. When she opened her own salon in New York's Fifth Avenue she searched for a more suitable name and was inspired by the book she was reading at the time called *Elizabeth and Her German Garden* by Elizabeth von Arnim, which contained verses from Tennyson's poem *Enoch Arden.*

Dorothy Gray was another American who opened a rival salon on Fifth Avenue, where she specialised in treatments for sensitive skins. Her massage treatments – which she carried out – were so popular that she insured her hands for a record US$100,000. Although Dorothy Gray's original skincare line has now disappeared, her name still appears on a range of toiletries made closer to home in Eastbourne, Sussex.

A longer-lived success story is that of Estée Lauder, one of the few women to become a legend in her own lifetime. Estée Lauder started up her business in 1946 by selling just four skincare products to the smart Saks Fifth Avenue department store in New York. From this humble beginning she founded the now world famous cosmetic company which she and her son Leonard still tightly control.

WARTIME REMEDIES

Back in Britain, however, the rigours of wartime rationing meant that there was very little in the way of glamorous make-up or beauty preparations. Women once again resorted to home remedies, including using gravy browning or strong tea to dye the legs in the absence of silk stockings. The restrictions on alcohol meant more concentrated perfumes and fewer eau de colognes were available and the lack of fats, oils and glycerine resulted in a shortage of skin creams.

Packaging was a problem for many manufacturers, with all the scrap metal being turned into munitions instead of make-up compacts. However, the beauty editor of *Queen* magazine did find time to mention Max Factor's Pan Cake make-up, recommending it 'particularly for women in the Forces or on other National work as it is very quick and easy to use and will stay on the skin for many hours . . . in six lovely shades from a pale flesh tint to a deep warm tan, in keeping with the colouring of the Woman's Service Uniforms.' A more important war-time purchaser of Pan Cake was the Ministry of Defence, who ordered specially formulated shades to darken the faces of commandos for night excursions.

After the war, developments in new cosmetics continued apace and throughout the fifties and sixties, make-up and skincare moved further away from Mother Nature and increasingly into the realms of technology. The concept of anti-ageing creams that might actually turn back the clock was introduced, together with its often ridiculously outlandish claims. Yet despite the catchy slogans and youthful models with artfully airbrushed skins, we have yet to encounter a skin cream that can cope with crow's feet.

In the last decade, the cosmetic and toiletry business has spent literally billions of dollars in search of the elusive elixir of youth that will wipe away all wrinkles. A whole variety of new ingredients have appeared on the scene, such as bovine collagen (made from cow fat), which claimed to be able to plump up the skin and give it a youthful appearance. The only problem with this is that the collagen molecules are far too large to penetrate even the uppermost layers of skin cells.

In a further refinement of technology, new 'delivery systems' were invented to carry complex ingredients into the skin where they might target ageing skin cells. Microscopically small liposomes were developed to slip through the surface of the skin where, in theory, they could release their cargo of active ingredients to individual skin cells. These active ingredients include a number of nutrients such as antioxidant vitamins, essential fatty acids, fruit acids and natural sugars.

Ironically, it has been the search for the most up-to-date and effective ingredients that has taken many cosmetic scientists back to nature's doorstep. Natural ingredients such as plant oils and herbal extracts, notably echinacea, are once again becoming increasingly popular as scientists begin to prove their legendary powers in the laboratory. Plant extracts such as chamomile have been found to heal damaged skin, avocado oil has been shown to regenerate ageing cells in mice and vitamins C and E are now known to be amongst the best anti-ageing ingredients of all times.

This is good news for us, as consumers. In fact, there has never been a better moment to combine the knowledge gathered by physicians, herbalists and beauticians over the last few thousand years and combine it with modern techniques to make the best natural beauty preparations for ourselves.

GETTING STARTED

The recipes for making your own natural beauty products are remarkably simple. You do not need to be a cosmetic scientist or have a degree in biotechnology to produce naturally effective products in your own kitchen. All the recipes have been tried and tested, but you may find some of the textures unusual. For example, the moisturising skin creams tend to be more concentrated than commercial lotions, as they have not been whipped with water and air to make them light. You may also find that some of the recipes vary according to the temperature, as ingredients such as coconut oil and cocoa butter are naturally harder in colder weather or if stored in a cool place.

This chapter lists the basic ingredients you will come across in the book, together with a description of how each one can be used. This means that you look up the properties of a particular ingredient and adapt a recipe to suit your own skin type, or devise your own concoctions in the future.

Many of the ingredients are probably sitting in your kitchen or bathroom right now. Others, such as herbs or fruits, can be grown in the garden or on a window sill to provide a year-round source of fresh ingredients. These are listed in more detail in The Botanicals chapter. If you have difficulty finding the more unusual ingredients, there is a list of stockists at the end of the book, as well as a glossary to explain the more technical terms.

USEFUL EQUIPMENT
Although there is little you need in the way of special equipment to start making your own beauty preparations, the following items will be helpful to have at hand. If you decide to make lots of your own recipes in the future, it might be worth keeping a set of utensils, such as spatulas, separate from the ones you use for cooking. This helps prevent the risk of cross-contamination of germs and odours, and means that your face cream will not end up smelling of onions!

- Plastic measuring spoons
- Set of small scales
- Heat-proof jugs or small bowls
- Enamel, stainless steel or Pyrex saucepan (not aluminium or cast iron, which can react with ingredients such as lemon juice)
- Fine mesh sieve
- Disposable coffee filters (to take tiny particles out of liquids)
- Small funnel for decanting liquids
- Rubber spatula or palette knife
- Metal mixing spoons (avoid wooden spoons, which absorb ingredients such as essential oils)
- Pipette (for measuring drop by drop, available from chemists)
Optional extras:
- Blender or food processor
- Pestle and mortar

The following are useful for packaging and storage:
- Selection of bottles and jars, preferably made from glass so they can be sterilised
- Sterilising fluid or tablets (from chemists)
- Spray bottles
- Paper towels (more hygienic than kitchen cloths for mopping up etc.)
- Sticky labels to name and date all items
- Cardboard boxes for storing finished items in the cool and dark (shoe boxes are ideal).

STORAGE TIPS
Unlike the needs of commercial beauty products, the recipes in this book do not contain added chemicals to prolong shelf-life. You will not find common skincare chemicals such as ethyl or isopropyl alcohols, parabens and ammonium compounds or benzoic acid

added to these natural remedies. However, steps must be taken to guard against bacterial or microbial spoilage and decomposition. Unfortunately, the basic oil and water mixture of many natural products is an excellent breeding ground for germs and a pot of cream is constantly exposed to new ones each time we dip our fingers into it.

Products most susceptible to spoilage include those made with fresh ingredients such as fruits and vegetables, although even these will usually keep for several days in the fridge. The quantities given for the recipes in this book are therefore designed to make relatively small amounts to avoid spoilage and subsequent wastage. Products stored in the fridge should be kept separate from food, such as in a salad drawer or in a cardboard box on the top shelf.

Make a habit of labelling every item with its name and the date of making so you know when to discard it. If in doubt — throw it out! Most skin creams can be safely stored in the bathroom cupboard, but keep them out of direct sunlight, which will encourage rancidity. A small disc of greaseproof paper placed on the top of each jar of cream helps to keep the air out and prolong shelf-life.

Adding vitamin E from capsules or from a few drops of wheatgerm oil also helps, as this nutrient acts as a natural preservative and prevents spoilage. Other natural preservatives include the antiseptic essential oils, notably lavender or menthol from peppermint, which have been added to beauty preparations for this reason for thousands of years.

HYGIENE HINTS

Bacteria love to breed in warm, moist conditions, so make life difficult for the bugs by keeping your equipment and preparation area as cool and dry as possible. All equipment, including final packing containers and lids, must be sterilised by dipping in sterilising fluid before using (alternatively, use a mild bleach solution and rinse well in boiled water). Whenever a recipe calls for water, only use filtered, boiled then cooled water, or distilled water, which is available from the chemist. Some varieties of bottled water may also be used, but choose reputable brands that have stringent quality controls and use those with low levels of minerals such as sodium (salt). Plain tap water contains many unwanted extras such as nitrates, chlorine, fluoride, traces of pesticides etc. and should not be used at all. It sounds obvious, but always wash your hands before you start.

ALLERGY TESTING

Most natural skincare remedies are well-suited to those with sensitive skins as they do not contain the artificial colourants and fragrances that most often lead to allergic reactions. Perfume contains as many as two hundred separate chemical ingredients, any one of which can trigger an adverse skin reaction. However, natural does not always equal safe and it is important to remember that even some completely natural substances can be dangerous if they are not handled with knowledge and care. Substances such as arsenic and lead are totally natural, yet we would not dream of using them on the skin. Likewise, many herbs and plant extracts have powerful effects that should not be underestimated, and must be treated with respect.

In the lists that follow you will find more detailed information on the safety of some of the stronger ingredients. Also, bear in mind that your own skin may not suit a particular ingredient or recipe. Although less likely to cause an allergic reaction than many chemical fragrances or preservatives, even basic natural ingredients such as lanolin or lemon juice can pose a problem for a few people. For this reason, it is wise to carry out a patch test whenever trying an ingredient or recipe for the first time.

HOW TO DO A PATCH TEST

Apply a small amount of the substance to be tested on an area of fine skin, such as the inner elbow. Cover with a sticking plaster and leave in place overnight. Should any unusual reaction, such as itching or redness, occur, bathe the affected area with a weak bicarbonate of soda solution and apply a soothing ointment such as calendula cream. Keep a record of the recipes you have tested and the ingredients which you know are suited to your skin. This will save time re-testing new products made with ingredients that you know are safe for your skin type.

RAW MATERIALS

The following A to Z of ingredients can be found in chemists or health shops:

Acetone

A harsh, colourless liquid that should be used with great care. It is highly flammable and is used as a thinner for paints and varnishes, including nail polish. It can be used sparingly as an inexpensive nail polish remover, but a small amount of almond oil should be added before use as it is extremely drying. Used in large amounts, acetone can cause skin rashes, and inhaling its pungent fumes can also irritate your lungs. However, small quantities of neat acetone can be carefully dabbed on to spots and pimples with a cotton bud as its drying action will remove any excess sebum or oil.

Aloe Vera Juice

This succulent African plant looks like a spineless cactus and is reputed to have been used by Cleopatra as a skin cleanser. It is a member of the lily family and has fat, rubbery green leaves which produce a thick, clear, semi-solid gel when cut. Aloe vera juice is made from the plant's natural gel and has been analysed as being 99·5 per cent water. However, the remaining 0·5 per cent contains over twenty different amino acids and carbohydrates, and many magical properties are credited to the plant's unusual juice. It contains a number of therapeutically active compounds including glycosides (a sugar derivative), polysaccharides (complex carbohydrate molecules) and volatile oils.

Aloe vera juice soothes and softens the skin and can help heal severe burns. It is a common ingredient in first-aid skin creams, shampoos and natural bodycare products. Studies at the University of Pennsylvania Radiology Department have found that the juice of this plant is more effective in treating radiation burns than any other known product. As a result, the American army have stockpiled significant quantities to be used on troops in the event of a nuclear disaster.

Aloe vera juice is available in bottles from health shops and can be added to tonics and cleansers to soothe the skin. The best quality juice or gel available contains 96-100 per cent pure aloe. Look for those that have not been preserved with alcohol as this diminishes the aloe's unique healing properties.

Almond Oil

This colourless plant oil is extracted from the oil-enriched kernels of sweet, ripe almonds grown mainly in the Mediterranean. It is an important ingredient in moisturising soaps, creams and skin treatments and can even be used neat as a nourishing hand and nail massage oil. A refined form of almond oil is available from the chemist, and some supermarkets also sell a gourmet version of the oil that is suitable for skincare use.

Arnica Tincture

Made from the dried flowers of the arnica plant, arnica has many uses in skincare. It is an efficient skin soother and is especially useful for drawing out bruises or easing aches and sprains. Used for centuries by homoeopaths, arnica tincture is one of our most effective remedies for sore, swollen skin, but should not be applied to scratches or open wounds (see The Botanicals, page 39).

Avocado Oil

This traditional beauty oil was first used by the tribeswomen of Mexico and Arizona where the avocado pear tree grows wild. The avocado itself is a highly unusual fruit as it takes two years to ripen and its flesh contains nearly fifty per cent plant oil. The natural oil is highly nutritious and is a good source of vitamin E, magnesium, traces of the B complex vitamins and lecithin. Although high in calories, the avocado does not contain any cholesterol and is a good source of the fatty acid linoleic acid, which strengthens the membranes surrounding skin cells. Its stone also contains as yet unidentified substances that have been shown in some studies to help regenerate skin cells.

Generally, the darker the avocado oil the better, as this means that it has undergone minimum processing and is likely to retain more of its natural nutrients. Avocado oil has a nutty smell and is one of the best oils for soothing dry, parched skins. It is available in either liquid form or capsules, which can be pierced with a pin and added to skin creams.

Balm of Gilead

This tincture is extracted from the buds of the poplar tree, common in Asia and North America. These reddish brown buds are coated with a sticky resin that is collected and made into Balm of Gilead. Its use as a skin-soothing ingredient and also as a pleasantly pungent perfume has been documented since biblical times. Balm of Gilead contains a type of painkiller called salicin which is also found in aspirin and is used in medical herbalism as an antiseptic and stimulant, especially when treating coughs and colds. The tincture is also a mild circulatory stimulant and can be used in skin lotions to tone and strengthen the epidermis or upper layers of the skin, although it should not be used near the eyes or mouth.

Borax

This white powder consists of alkaline crystals and comes from a mineral that is mined in North and South America. It is a form of the trace mineral boron, which is used by the body to keep bones and teeth healthy and strong. Commonly used as a water softener, preservative and skin soother, borax also acts as an antiseptic, although it should not be used on broken skin. Borax has soothing properties and is used in many beauty products including soaps, shampoos, eye gels and moisturisers. It also has mild emulsifying properties which is why it is included in some of my natural skin cream recipes.

Calamine Lotion

This old-fashioned skin lotion is made from the rhizome or root of the sweet flag plant *Acorus calamus*. Calamine lotion also contains zinc oxide, with five per cent iron oxide added to turn the liquid a pale pink colour. The liquid has drying and cooling properties and is useful for sore, sunburnt skin. It can also be found in astringent skin tonics and some facial washes.

Castor Oil

Extracted from the castor bean plant that grows in India, Canada and North America, this is a colourless or yellow oil which is pressed from the beans. These beans are poisonous, but the toxic protein ricin is left behind in the mulch after pressing. Purified castor oil is used in hairdressings such as brilliantine to give the hair a glossy shine, and in waxy cosmetics such as lipsticks. It is a useful cosmetic ingredient as it leaves a shiny film on the surface of the hair and skin, and also acts as a waterproofing agent for barrier and nappy rash creams. Castor oil rarely causes a reaction on the skin.

Cocoa Butter

This is the solid fat made from the roasted seeds of the cocoa tree. These seeds also give us chocolate and cocoa, and cocoa butter itself has a naturally sweet, chocolatey smell.

The cocoa tree was first discovered in the sixteenth century by a Spanish explorer visiting the South American country of Mexico. He brought the cocoa bean back to Europe where it was processed into a sweet, chocolatey drink. It was not until the nineteenth century that the beauty benefits of the cocoa bean were fully realised. In 1828, the invention of the cocoa press made it possible to squeeze and filter the ground beans, extracting a liquid cocoa butter and leaving a dry low-fat cake of cocoa. This process signalled the start of the chocolate industry as we know it today and also introduced us to cocoa butter as a moisturiser.

One of its most notable properties is that it melts at body temperature, and is therefore good for rubbing into the skin. Cocoa butter is a useful body moisturiser and also has the reputation for helping prevent stretchmarks.

Coconut Oil

This semi-solid plant oil looks more like cream; it is so full of saturated fat it solidifies at room temperature. Coconut oil comes from the dried flesh of the coconut which contains around sixty-five per cent natural oil. It is often added to cosmetics and toiletries as it does not go rancid easily and is a good natural cleansing agent. It has low-lathering detergent properties and can be used to make shampoos and gentle washing-up liquids. The oil is also commonly added to soaps and body lotions. It can be used on its own as an effective skin moisturiser, or mixed with a few drops of sandalwood oil to make a fragrant hair shiner.

Emulsifying Ointment

This is a useful skincare ingredient sold by most chemists. It is a mixture of parafin wax, liquid parafin and emulsifying wax, and is commonly used by those who are allergic or sensitive to ordinary soap. Although the ointment contains bland mineral oils, it is a useful ingredient in small quantities for binding skin creams and other semi-solid moisturisers.

Evening Primrose Oil

The evening primrose is a tall, spiky plant with vivid yellow flowers that bloom in the evening, hence its name. It is not related to the common primrose but to the bay willow herb, and its oil comes from thousands of tiny, dark brown seeds. Although the origins of the evening primrose can be traced back by fossil remains to some 70,000 years ago, it is only recently that skincare scientists have been taking this unusual flower seriously. The secret to the plant's success is its oil which has an unusual fatty acid composition.

All oils contain essential fatty acids which are good for the skin both internally and externally; however, evening primrose oil contains a type of essential fatty acid known as gamma linolenic acid (GLA). Evening primrose oil contains about nine per cent pure GLA, which is an unusually large percentage. The only other sources of GLA are blackcurrant seeds, borage oil and human breast milk. Borage oil itself is a richer source of GLA than evening primrose oil, but more difficult to find. GLA has been found to be helpful when taken in capsule form for treating hormonal problems such as PMS, symptoms of the menopause and for controlling eczema.

Evening primrose oil can also be rubbed into patches of eczema to aid the healing process and may be added to moisturising creams to enrich them. Many skincare ranges now add evening primrose oil to their products, but generally they use such tiny quantities that their value on the skin is questionable. A more effective method is to make your own creams using higher quantities of this natural oil. The easiest way to obtain evening primrose oil is to pierce a capsule with a pin and squeeze out its contents. Alternatively, the oil is also available in a dropper bottle for more accurate measuring.

Fuller's Earth

This is sold in small packets and looks like powdered clay. In fact, Fuller's earth is mined from reclaimed areas of the seabed, where it is created from the remains of single-cell algae laid down over millions of years.

It is so-called because fullers have used it for centuries to extract the natural grease or lanolin from sheep's wool. The fuller was an important member of the textile industry, whose job was to make the cloth heavier or more compact during manufacture by shrinking and beating or pressing.

Fuller's earth itself is a highly absorbent cosmetic ingredient and works by drawing out dirt and embedded impurities from the skin. This makes it good for recipes such as deep-cleansing face and body packs. Fuller's earth is also a rich natural source of silica, an important mineral for maintaining skin strength and suppleness.

Glycerine

Most glycerine is extracted from animal fat, although some vegetable glycerine is becoming more widely available from herbal suppliers. The better brands of skincare products also contain vegetable glycerine, although it is more expensive than the animal version. The glycerine that is sold in chemists shops is made when animal fat or lard is heated industrially and a sticky, colourless liquid siphoned off. Glycerine mixes well with both water and alcohol and is an efficient skin softener. It is a humectant, which means that it attracts water. This makes it useful for attracting moisture from the atmosphere into the skin, but an excess can also draw out the skin's own natural water content and lead to dryness. It is used in making clear soaps and other skin soothers, such as moisturisers and aftershave balms.

Henna

This natural pigment comes from the henna plant, which is native to Egypt, the Middle East and India. Made from powdered leaves and stems of the shrub, henna is a natural hair and skin dye. The henna is mixed with water to form a paste to dye the hair various shades of red or brown. The drawback with using natural henna is that the results can be unpredictable and it should only be used after carrying out a patch test to establish the shade of the finished result. Henna should be kept away from the eyes and should not be used to dye either eyelashes or eyebrows. Henna leaves are also used occasionally by herbalists for their astringent and anti-bacterial qualities.

Hydrogen Peroxide

This colourless liquid has powerful bleaching and antiseptic properties. It is commonly used in the cosmetic industry as a preservative. A three per cent solution can be bought from the chemist and used medicinally as an antiseptic and germicide. Useful for dabbing neat on to spots, pimples and boils, hydrogen peroxide should not be used on sensitive areas of mucous membrane such as the eyes, nose and mouth.

Jojoba Oil

Pronounced 'ho-ho-ba', this pale yellow oil is, in fact, a liquid wax that comes from the seeds of the evergreen jojoba plant grown mainly in Mexico. Traditionally used by the Aztecs and the Mexican Indians, jojoba oil is another of Mother Nature's beauty assets and remains an important ingredient in many modern scalp and skin lotions. Jojoba oil is unusual because it is the only wax that is naturally liquid at room temperature. It is very similar in chemical composition to sperm whale oil, called spermaceti, which was wide-ly used in skincare creams until the early eighties. Jojoba oil also closely matches the skin's own oil, called sebum, and this makes it a good oil to use in facial treatments, especially for oily skins. Another benefit is that jojoba has a lengthy shelf-life and, unlike most other vegetable oils, does not spoil when left open to the air and sunlight.

Kaolin

Also known as China clay, kaolin originated from the Kaoling Hills in Southeast China. Kaolin is a pure type of clay and can be used in beauty recipes instead of Fuller's earth. Kaolin is now mined in many parts of the world, notably Cornwall, China and Japan (where it is used to make their traditional chalky-white face powders). It is highly absorbent and attracts moisture and for this reason it is found in many talcum powders and deodorants. It is also used in many remedies for diarrhoea, such as kaolin and morphine, and is also an important ingredient in deep-cleansing face packs and abrasive tooth powders.

Lanolin

Chemically speaking, lanolin is a wax, not a fat, although it is often described as the natural fat found in sheep's wool — produced by the animal to provide an extra layer of insulation against harsh winters. Most fleeces contain around twenty per cent lanolin. Lanolin can be safely extracted after the sheep have been sheared, and does not involve killing the sheep. Lanolin is extracted by dipping the fleece into alcohol to dissolve the fats present, or scrubbing the fleece in soap.

As an ingredient, lanolin sinks into the skin easily and is a useful moisturiser. A few may be allergic to lanolin, but most allergic reactions come from other ingredients found in cosmetics such as synthetic fragrances and preservatives. A bland, purified lanolin cream is available from most chemists and is a useful ingredient for many skin-soothing recipes.

Magnesia

This alkaline white powder is named after the ancient city of Magnesia in Asia Minor. Often added to stomach upset remedies, it has a drying and tightening effect on the skin. Useful for dabbing neat on to spots and pimples, magnesia can also be found in skin fresheners, anti-perspirants and talcum powders.

Mineral Oil

Made from highly refined petroleum, mineral oil is found in baby oils, baby lotions and commercial cold creams. Unfortunately, when it is heated it give off a distinctive petrol aroma. A pure, bland product with a lengthy shelf-life, mineral oil crops up in literally thousands of cosmetic and toiletry preparations. It leaves a characteristic film on the skin and does not penetrate the surface. Some dermatologists advise sensitive and acne-prone patients to avoid mineral oil as it can cause an allergic reaction on the skin. Plant oils, such as avocado oil, can be used instead, as these sink more deeply into the skin and contain more nourishing ingredients such as natural vitamins and moisturising essential fatty acids.

Orris Root

This fragrant root or rhizome is an important ingredient in perfume-making as it is used as a fixative for fine fragrances. Orris root comes from the dried rhizome of the *Iris florentina* and is an expensive commodity. This is because it takes four years to grow the rhizomes and two more years to dry them out before they can be used. Ground orris root is useful as a natural talcum pow-

der and a dry hair shampoo. It can also be added to home-made pot-pourri blends as a perfume fixative.

Petroleum Jelly

Also known as petrolatum, this jelly is produced as a by-product of the petroleum industry and is obtained by treating petrol with steam and filtering at high temperatures. Technically, petroleum jelly is a purified mixture of semi-solid hydrocarbons from petroleum. Some may also have an understandable aversion to putting a by-product of petrol on to their skin. Petroleum jelly is extremely thick and works well as a barrier cream, lip salve or a base for home-made ointments.

Pumice

This grey stone consists mainly of silicates and can be found on the beaches of most Greek islands. It has abrasive properties and is used in tooth whiteners, skin scrubs and cleansing grains. Natural pumice stones are often sold to remove the dead, hardened skin on the soles of the feet. These stones are made when the pumice solidifies into small grey lumps thrown out from the many active volcanoes in and around Greece.

Rhassoul Mud

This fine, powdered clay comes from Morocco, where it is mined in the Atlas Mountains. It is useful for its de-greasing properties and can be added to hair and body packs to remove excess dirt and sebum. It can also be added to scalp treatments to help severe cases of dandruff and flaking scalps and works by drawing out impurities from the hair follicles. Dried Rhassoul mud is available in small packets from healthfood shops and herbal suppliers, and is a useful substitute for other types of powdered clays such as kaolin or Fuller's earth.

Wheatgerm Oil

Another important beautycare ingredient, wheatgerm oil is our richest natural source of vitamin E. It comes from the seed or 'germ' of the wheat stalk and is also rich in many vitamins and essential fatty acids that strengthen the skin. Wheatgerm oil is rich and sticky and too concentrated to use on its own or for massage, but a small amount can be added to skin creams and lotions. In addition to enriching a recipe, wheatgerm oil also acts as a natural preservative and its vitamin E content will prevent the cream from becoming rancid.

Wheatgerm oil is also one of the best anti-ageing ingredients as its high vitamin E content helps neutralise the destructive particles known as free radicals within the skin. These elements are responsible for most of the skin's visible signs of premature ageing, including loss of skin tone and wrinkles. Wheatgerm oil has a distinctive, nutty aroma which you either love or loathe. Either way, a few drops added to skin creams and massage oil blends make one of the most useful of all beauty ingredients.

Zinc Oxide

This thick white paste was the original total sunblock and it can still be used to screen out virtually all of the sun's harmful rays. Zinc oxide has astringent properties, and also dries the skin. It can help healing and is often found in nappy rash creams, anti-perspirants and shaving creams.

FROM THE KITCHEN CUPBOARD
The following ingredients are from the kitchen cupboard:

Arrowroot

This culinary thickener is used in soups, sauces and gravies but also crops up in talcum powders and hair dyes. Arrowroot comes from the starchy roots of a tropical plant that is common in the West Indies. It was first used by native American Indians to heal wounds inflicted by poisoned arrows. Nowadays, arrowroot is added to moisturisers to make them thicker and to help the active ingredients penetrate the upper levels of the skin.

Beeswax

Commonly found in furniture polish, beeswax also plays an important role in keeping our complexion polished and protected. Beeswax comes from the hexagonal honeycombs in which bees store their honey and flower pollen. Each hexagonal cell is sealed with a fine sheet of beeswax to protect and preserve the honey inside.

Beeswax itself is used in many cosmetic preparations, such as moisturising creams, mascara and other kinds of make-up. It has a thick, waxy texture and is good for using on chapped areas of exposed skin, such as the hands and lips. It is available either in small honey-coloured blocks from healthfood shops, or as easy-to-melt granules for cosmetic and candle-making, sold by a herbal supplier. Beeswax acts as a natural emulsifyer and is a useful ingredient in moisturising skin creams.

Brewer's Yeast

This vitamin-enriched food supplement is an excellent source of the important B vitamins, especially thiamin, riboflavin and nicotinic acid. Brewer's yeast is often added to face masks and hair packs for its deeply nourishing properties. It tends to be expensive if bought in capsule form, but it is much cheaper and convenient to use packets of dried brewer's yeast from healthfood shops. It is a useful ingredient in beauty recipes, especially for enriching face masks and moisturising creams.

Carrageen Moss

Technically a seaweed, this is also known as Irish moss as it grows mainly around the west coast of Ireland. It has powerful gelling properties and crops up in countless cosmetic preparations, from toothpaste to toilet soap. Carrageen moss contains a type of ingredient known in herbalism as a mucilage, meaning that it can be made into a jelly or thick paste. For this reason it is used to thicken many skin creams, gels and face masks. The mucilage in carrageen moss helps relieve skin irritations by forming a protective layer over delicate mucous membranes, and can rapidly relieve inflammation. Medical herbalists may also use carrageen moss internally to treat persistent coughs or peptic (stomach) ulcers. Dehydrated carrageen moss is available from some supermarkets and health shops.

Cornflour

Also known as cornstarch, this is made from finely ground maize or sweetcorn kernels and often crops up in talcum powder and fine face powder. Highly absorbent, it is useful as a home-made anti-perspirant and can be used on its own or blended with arrowroot.

Corn Oil

This vegetable oil is extracted from ripened corn kernels, and is also known as maize oil. Unrefined corn oil, from healthfood shops, contains high levels of vitamin E, which make it a useful body moisturiser. Corn oil is thicker than most other vegetable oils and should be used sparingly to prevent stickiness.

Gelatine

This jelling agent is obtained by boiling the skin, tendons, ligaments and bones of animal carcasses with water. Gelatine attracts moisture and is able to absorb between five to ten times its own weight in water. It is used in protein shampoos because it gives the hair more 'body', and is also the main ingredient in peel-off face masks and some fingernail strengtheners. Carageen moss may be used as an alternative, vegetable-based gelling agent.

Grapeseed Oil

Grapeseed oil is a light, colourless oil that is extracted from grape pips. Because it is highly refined, grapeseed oil has a fine texture and is odourless, making it one of the best plant oils for massage. Many aromatherapists use grapeseed oil to blend with essential oils before massage treatments. Grapeseed oil is also a useful ingredient of body lotions and lightweight skin creams.

Groundnut Oil

Also known as peanut oil, this oil comes from peanut kernels. The peanut is not actually a nut, but the seed pod of a legume that grows beneath the ground. Common in Africa, India and China, peanuts are a rich source of protein and produce a nutritious oil that is a valuable source of vitamin E. Unrefined groundnut oil, from healthfood shops, is the best type to use in beauty recipes as this retains most of its natural nutrients.

Hazelnut Oil

One of the newest plant oils to appear on the supermarket shelves, hazelnut oil is made from pressed hazelnut kernels. The best quality oil comes from France, where much of it is still produced in old-fashioned, family-run oil mills. Hazelnut oil has good penetrating powers and is one of the best oils to use on the skin. Pharmacist Claudine Luu, who runs courses on natural medicine at Montpelier University in the South of France, recommends using hazelnut oil as a base for essential oil massage. She says it is especially good for treating conditions such as abscesses, acne and sore throats, where the essential oils are required to quickly penetrate the surface of the skin.

Honey

Made by bees from the sweet nectar in plants and flowers, honey itself is a mixture of ninety-eight per cent sugars, with two per cent enzymes, vitamins and minerals. It has mildly antiseptic properties, meaning that bacterium cannot survive in it. There are several different types of honey, and its colour is largely affected by the kinds of blossom that the bees visit to produce it. The best-quality honey is also slightly cloudy, which means that it retains the vitamin-enriched pollen that contributes to its nutrient content. The darker-coloured honeys have higher levels of minerals and are probably better to use in skincare recipes. Honey is a useful soothing ingredient in moisturisers, hand creams and body lotions, but it is best avoided if you are allergic to pollen or grasses.

Kelp

Also known as bladderwrack, kelp is often used as a generic name for all kinds of seaweed and can be found in most good healthfood shops. Dehydrated kelp can be bought in packets to use as a vegetable, or in powder form, either loose or in capsules. It should not be used fresh from the beach unless you are sure that the waters from which it came are unpolluted.

Rich in vitamins and marine minerals, kelp is a useful ingredient in face masks and treatments for several skin problems, including psoriasis. As with carrageen moss, another type of seaweed, kelp is rich in mucilage or gelling agents. It is widely used by medical herbalists to treat sluggishness and joint inflammations such as arthritis. It is also used for thyroid conditions because of its high iodine content and is known as the slimmer's friend, as it stimulates thyroid activity which in turn peps up a sluggish metabolism.

Lecithin

Lecithin is an essential fatty acid found in egg yolks, soya beans, avocados and unrefined cooking oils. In humans, lecithin is found in the membranes of all our cells and it is a vital component of skin tissue, helping to keep the complexion strong and healthy. One of the easiest ways to use lecithin in cosmetic recipes is in the form of egg yolks, which contain around ten per cent pure lecithin. It can also be bought in powdery granules or in capsules from a chemist or healthfood shop.

Lecithin is one of the skin's own Natural Moisturising Factors (NMFs) which are found in the lower levels of the skin. Other NMFs include urea compounds, lactic acid and glycolic acid. Lecithin acts as an emulsifier, holding a liquid in a suspension to prevent it separating. This is why egg yolks are used in making mayonnaise – to bind together the oil and vinegar. Lecithin is a useful skincare ingredient and is often added to moisturisers, as it helps lock moisture into the skin.

Linseeds
Also known as flaxseeds, these come from the flax plant, which used to be a common sight in Britain during Anglo-Saxon times when it was grown to produce flax linen. The seeds themselves are small, brown and shiny, and have an oily taste, due to their extremely high natural oil content. Linseeds are rich in mucilage and waxes and can be used to make natural gels and thick pastes for beauty recipes. Linseeds can also be used internally as a safe, effective remedy for constipation, and make good internal cleansers (simply swallow a handful followed by a large glass of water to encourage the seeds to swell up and pass quickly through the digestive tract). Medical herbalists use linseeds internally to relieve rasping coughs or to draw out boils and other types of severe skin inflammations. Linseeds may also be used in poultices to heal burns, scalds and boils.

Maple Syrup
Natural maple syrup comes from the sap of the Canadian maple tree *Acer saccarum*. It is a natural source of sugars that are similar to those needed by the skin to maintain its moisture content. Pure maple syrup (not to be confused with the more common synthetic version) has moisturising and slightly antiseptic properties, and can be used in recipes instead of honey.

Oatmeal
Oats are a good source of protein, vitamins and, perhaps surprisingly, polyunsaturated fats. They are also extremely soothing on the skin and are perfect ingredients for treating overly dry, irritated or sensitive skin conditions. There are several different types of oatmeal that may be used successfully in skincare recipes and all are available from supermarkets or healthfood shops. Porridge oat flakes are useful for adding to a warm bath to soften the water and help restore moisture to the skin. Coarsely ground and medium ground oatmeal make good exfoliating skin scrubs, while fine ground oatmeal is better for treatments on areas of more delicate skin, such as the face and neck.

Olive Oil
Not only is olive oil the best type of oil for cooking, it is also an essential ingredient of many beauty recipes. One reason is that, unlike other vegetable oils, olive oil remains stable when heated to high temperatures and

also resists rancidity. Olive oil has been used in skincare for thousands of years (the father of medicine, Hippocrates, said that it should be rubbed on to sunburn to help heal inflamed skin).

There are two main types of olive oil that you can buy from the supermarket. Extra virgin oil is the best quality, as it contains the first pressing of the olives and has not been chemically refined. In fact, this is one of the few truly natural ingredients still found on the supermarket shelves. Extra virgin olive oil contains the most vitamin E and lecithin. Its disadvantage is that it also has a distinctive, olivey smell which can be off-putting. Pure olive oil, also sold by chemists as a liquid laxative, is often a better choice for beauty recipes, as it is more refined with a fine texture and little fragrance. Highly purified olive oil is also available from the chemist, and this may be used if you want to avoid all traces of odour.

Propolis

This has been around for 58 million years (as long as the bee!) and is another by-product of the industrious honey makers. Propolis is the brown, gum-like substance that bees make by collecting sap from tree buds and mix with their own secretions to paint the inside of their hives and mummify the remains of any intruders. The famous Greek physician Hippocrates used propolis for skin ulcers, both internal and external.

Propolis is highly antiseptic and has remarkable anti-bacterial properties which repel bacterial and fungal infections on the skin. It is also reputed to strengthen the human immune system by encouraging the thymus gland to produce extra white blood cells. Propolis contains flavonoids which have antioxidant properties and help fight the destructive effects of free radicals within the skin. Some flavonoids are known to be anti-inflammatory and may even be able to boost collagen production within the skin. Propolis also contains ferucic acid which has a strong, natural antibiotic effect on the skin.

Propolis is increasingly used in skincare for treating problems such as acne, and propolis cream combined with propolis tablets or capsules can be helpful in some cases of eczema. Propolis ointment can also be used to treat bruises, cuts, frostbite, chilblains, burns and also skin ulcers. This versatile natural ingredient has mild painkilling properties and can also be found in health shops in the form of a spray for a sore throat, or soothing lozenges.

Rice Flour

A fine, creamy-coloured flour made from ground rice, this has an unusually silky texture. Highly absorbent and drying on the skin, rice flour is often used in face and body powders and is available from good health-food shops. Pure rice flour is a useful substitute for talcum powder and can be scented with the addition of a few drops of aromatic essential oils.

Royal Jelly

Royal jelly is made by the worker bees as food to fatten up the queen bee and sustain her supply of larvae. As worker bees live for about six weeks and the queen can live for up to six years (despite laying around 2000 eggs a day), royal jelly is obviously powerful stuff. Little is known about the exact attributes of this remarkable substance. Technically, royal jelly contains traces of all the B vitamins, vitamin C, twenty-two amino acids, numerous minerals, enzymes and trace elements, plus a mysterious four per cent which has defied analysis. Royal jelly is often added to skincare ranges and is said to have miraculous anti-ageing properties, although the tiny amounts added to commercial skincare products means it would have minimal effect. While it is unlikely that royal jelly will turn back the clock, it may help to reduce dryness and sensitivity to some skin types. It can be bought in capsule form and the contents of these are a useful ingredient for adding to face masks and enriching skin creams.

Sesame Oil
One of the earliest plant oils to be used in health and beauty remedies, sesame oil can be traced back to Roman times. The oil comes from the plant's tiny seeds, which themselves are a good source of iron, calcium and protein. Sesame oil is soothing on the skin and has little or no smell, making it a good choice for many natural beauty recipes.

Sunflower Oil
This popular vegetable oil comes from the seeds in the head of the sunflower plant, which is grown throughout America and Europe for its valuable oil. An attractive, fast-growing plant, sunflowers can also be grown in the garden. Once the seeds have ripened and turned black they can be collected and eaten as a nutritious snack. The vivid yellow flower petals may also be dried and used to make a natural blonde hair dye. Sunflower oil is best bought in an unrefined state from a healthfood shop, as this contains higher levels of nutrients, including vitamin E and calcium. It is a useful and inexpensive basic oil for massage blends and body lotions.

Walnut Oil
An expensive oil that contains high levels of vitamin E and other useful skin nutrients, walnut oil is sometimes known by its French name *huile de noix*. Walnut oil can be found in healthfood shops or on some supermarket shelves. It is made from warm-pressing walnut kernels, which are naturally rich in this golden oil. Walnut oil can be used in skincare blends and is a useful alternative to almond or hazelnut oil.

Vanilla Pods
These long dark beans are a member of the orchid family and can be found on the shelves of delicatessens and healthfood shops. Vanilla pods have been valued for their exotic fragrance for centuries and were first used by the Aztecs to fragrance body creams and perfumes. The pods are very expensive but can be used again and again to give a warm, subtle aroma to skincare recipes. Whenever you use a pod, rinse it well, dry thoroughly and return to an airtight container. Alternatively, a few drops of natural vanilla essence will give a similar velvety scent to products like body lotions and hand creams.

Vinegar
Each country develops its own type of vinegar according to the local alcoholic drinks — wine vinegars in France, rice vinegars in Japan and malt vinegar based on beer in Britain. Although it is our home-brew, malt vinegar should not be used on the skin as it is far too harsh, and overpoweringly pungent. The best form of vinegar for skincare products, such as skin tonics, is natural cider vinegar which has a relatively low acidity. Cider vinegar contains around five per cent malic acid, which is similar to the hydrochloric acid produced by the stomach and used to digest food. Cider vinegar is useful for restoring the correct acid pH balance to skin fresheners and for adding to the final rinsing water after shampooing to

THE
BOTANICALS

In addition to the basic range of raw materials needed to make preparations to cleanse and protect our skin and hair, there is also a growing range of natural plant extracts that can be added to give products specific benefits. For example, a skin tonic may be created to suit a dry, sensitive skin by adding chamomile flowers, or a product may be made suitable for an oily, combination skin by including nettles and yarrow.

Herbal extracts are ideal for 'customising' a beauty recipe and adding a personal touch to skin creams or massage blends. You may also have a particular scent that you are fond of, such as rose or lavender, and these may be added to many of my recipes in the form of a few drops of fragrant essential oil.

PLANTS AND HERBS

The Romans were largely responsible for bringing many Mediterranean plants and herbs to Britain and for their subsequent wide-scale cultivation. They encouraged the use of plants and herbs in health and beauty preparations, as well as in perfumes and as salad or cooking ingredients. After the Roman Empire collapsed, herbs and herbal medicines fell out of favour, encouraged by the rise of Christianity which considered faith, penitence and prayer to be the only answers to illness. Herbs then became associated with witchcraft and many of the original herbalists had a difficult time in re-establishing their art.

However, many herbs and plants remain potent natural healers and have a wide range of uses in beauty preparations. For example, a variety of bullwort has been used for centuries for skin and kidney complaints, and it is now used in hospitals, together with ultraviolet light therapy, to treat severe skin conditions such as psoriasis and vitiligo. Even on a day-to-day level most modern skincare products still rely on herbal extracts that have been tried and tested over thousands of years.

The simplest way to ensure a steady supply of fresh herbs and plants, such as roses and geraniums, is to grow your own, either in the garden, in a window box or along a sunny window sill. Many extracts come from plants normally classed as weeds, such as stinging nettles, and these are remarkably easy to grow. In fact, without careful control, they will quickly take over the flowerbeds. Many flowers also have unusual properties that are especially useful in skincare. For example, marigolds give us a soothing calendula extract and geranium leaves contain one of the best natural perfumes.

When picking herbs and wild plants, avoid those that have been growing along a roadside or close to any source of industrial pollution. Plants are highly sensitive to pollutants in the atmosphere and quickly absorb them into their petals and leaves. If growing or gathering your own supplies sounds too much like hard work, dried herbs and flower heads are readily available from herbal suppliers (there is a list of these at the back of this book). Fresh herbs are also increasingly available from supermarkets and greengrocers, but do not be tempted to use flowers from the florist as these blooms are often sprayed with powerful herbicides which will harm the skin.

The most useful plants for cosmetic and beauty preparations are alphabetically listed on the following pages.

ARNICA *Arnica montana*

Also known as leopard's bane, this vivid yellow alpine flower has many well-documented medicinal uses. The arnica flower looks like a spindly yellow daisy, but it is the plant's roots that are of most use to us. From the root we can extract tincture of arnica, a powerful compound containing the bitter yellow substance called arnicin. Unlike its flowers, the root also contains tannins as well as several minerals. Tincture of arnica is available from most chemists and is extremely useful for applying to bruises (every first-aid kit should contain a bottle). It works by stimulating the circulation, and arnica cream is one of the most effective remedies for preventing a bruise from turning blue. I use a homoeopathic arnica cream almost daily on my children's bumps and bruises. Tincture of arnica is toxic, so it is for external use only and must not be swallowed. However, an extremely diluted form of arnica as tablets is available from homoeopathic suppliers and this is an excellent remedy for shock, or any emotional or physical injury. A safe, highly effective treatment, arnica tablets are especially recommended for children's tumbles, childbirth and minor accidents. See page 140 for details of homoeopathic suppliers and practitioners.

CHAMOMILE (German) *Matricaria chamomilla*

This herb takes its name from the Greek *kamai* (ground) and *melon* (apple) because of the sweet apple-like fragrance it releases when trodden on. Traditionally used to make scented lawns, chamomile is a low-growing, ground-covering herb with many practical uses. There are many varieties, but aromatherapists prefer *Matricaria chamomilla*, or German chamomile, which produces a highly prized blue oil.

The secret to this plant's success are substances called azulenes which have skin-soothing and anti-inflammatory properties. Natural azulenes are also believed to relieve pain, improve skin tissues and stimulate the immune-boosting activity of white blood cells. Azulenes can also found in the herb yarrow (see page 48).

Natural German chamomile also contains another extract called alpha-bisabolol, which is used in many skincare preparations for its uniquely soothing action on the skin. Studies at the University of Bonn in Germany have shown alpha-bisabolol to have both painkilling and anti-inflammatory properties. Trials have illustrated that it helps repair sun-damaged and chemically injured skin tissues, and that there is a proven basis for using chamomile extract to help wound healing.

The medicinal properties of natural chamomile are concentrated in the yellow centre of its flowers, and this is the part that is dried and turned into a sedative herb tea. Other parts of the plant, such as the whole flower heads and the leaves, are useful as a tonic and can be added to a bath to relieve tired, aching muscles.

Chamomile flowers are also useful as a gentle hair dye and bring a glossy sheen to naturally blonde hair. Chamomile tea-bags are a useful and convenient way of making herbal infusions and also make a soothing drink that helps the digestion. Medical herbalists often use chamomile internally to treat tension headaches, insomnia and nervous digestive disorders. The herb is also used frequently in children's remedies as it can help to calm and relieve many infant conditions including colic, teething and hyperactivity. Pure chamomile concentrate is available in liquid form from healthfood shops for adding to skincare recipes or using in healing compresses.

CHRYSANTHEMUM *Chrysanthemum morifolium*

This popular garden flower is cultivated in China purely for its medicinal properties. Herbalism has been popular in the Far East for at least the last 5000 years and relies on Oriental herbs and plants for its medicines. The principle of this form of herbalism is prevention rather than cure by achieving an internal yin-yang balance (where the body is in a state of perfect harmony with no sign of stress or strain). The idea of yin and yang was developed around 100 BC by Dong Zhongshu. He documented the balance of opposing principles (yin-yang) as applied to the body. 'Cold' herbs and foods (yin) were identified to correct 'hot' conditions or diseases, and vice versa. The principles of balancing foods in this way is still practised today by most of China's one billion inhabitants.

Chrysanthemum petals contain useful essential oils which have sedative and soothing properties. In Chinese medicine they are prescribed for headaches, influenza, hypertension and atherosclerosis (hardening of the arteries). An infusion is used as an eye bath for disorders such as conjunctivitis and it is used in compresses to treat abscesses. An infusion can be made using fresh flower heads or chrysanthemum tea bags (from health shops) and makes an astringent skin tonic. Chrysanthemum tea combines many of the soothing benefits of drinking chamomile tea, but tastes better because it does not contain the glycoside called anthemic acid that gives chamomile its slightly bitter taste.

COMFREY *Symphytum officinale*

A tall herb that is best suited to growing outdoors in the back of a flower bed or in the vegetable patch, comfrey is the friend of the organic gardener. Russian comfrey or the *Symphytum perigrinum* variety is often grown specifically to be turned into a nutrient-rich compost for fertilising the soil. Comfrey contains many vitamins, minerals and trace elements that are ideal for replenishing nutrients in the earth. It also contains allantoin, which is extracted from its roots and used as an effective skin soother and healer. For this reason, allantoin extracts are often added to ointments to help eczema and psoriasis. Comfrey is also used to heal wounds, stomach ulcers and bone fractures as it contains agents that bind tissues while also stimulating new growth.

CORNFLOWER *Centaurea cyanus*

A plant that likes to grow in or near cornfields, hence its name, the cornflower is easily recognised by its vivid blue flowers. The petals provide a deep blue dye that is used to make ink and water-colour paints. Cornflower extract also comes from its blue petals and has mildly antibiotic properties which are used to soothe the skin. An infusion of flower heads in distilled water makes a mildly astringent skin tonic. Cornflower lotions are also especially soothing around the eye area and the extract is often added to expensive eye creams.

COWSLIP *Primula veris*

A small wild flower with a tall stem topped with a dozen or so vivid yellow blooms, the cowslip plant has a sweet smell, due to the anethol content in its stems and roots. Its name comes from the Anglo Saxon *cusloppe*, meaning cow's slobber. Cowslip has been used in medical herbalism for centuries for its stimulating expectorant, anti-spasmodic and sedative properties. It is still possible to buy herbal cough mixtures containing cowslip extracts, which are especially useful to treat children with bronchitis or whooping cough. The flowers are also useful in skincare for sensitive skins.

DANDELION *Taraxacum officinale*

This plant gets its name from the French words for lion's tooth *dent de lion*. It was given this nickname by ancient herbalists who considered it to be as powerful as the teeth of the lion when it comes to tackling disorders of the human body. Dandelion leaves are highly nutritious and one of our richest sources of iron and potassium, and numerous other vitamins and minerals. Instead of spraying the dandelions in your lawn with weed-killer, pick the leaves when they are young and tender and add them to a salad. The leaves can be covered by a bucket while they are still growing, to blanch them and reduce their bitterness. The leaves may also be dried and made into a tea, which has mild diuretic properties.

Dandelion root is also highly prized by medical herbalists as a digestive, a liver tonic and a natural laxative. It is also used to treat skin problems such as eczema and inflammation, and conditions including jaundice. In addition, the white sap from the plant's stalks is reputed to be an effective long-term remedy for removing warts.

EYEBRIGHT *Euphrasia officinalis*

A small pretty plant with dainty dark green leaves and bluish white flowers, eyebright is an alpine herb that rarely grows taller than 18 cm (7in) high. Eyebright always grows on grass, which it relies on for providing part of its food supply. It is so-called due to its effectiveness at clearing the eyes and preventing soreness.

The homoeopathic tincture of euphrasia is excellent for treating eye disorders such as conjunctivitis, or swollen, sticky eyes associated with hay fever and allergies. To use, dilute one drop in a sterile eye-bath with distilled or boiled, cooled water. Use to bathe the eyes three times a day, using a different eye-bath for each eye to prevent cross infection. As homemade infusions of eye-bright may not be sufficiently sterile to use directly in the eyes, it is best to use tincture of euphrasia or a professional liquid decoction of the herb. Eyebright may also be used in compresses to relieve tired, red eye and is often added to commercial eye drops and gels for this reason.

Eyebright is naturally rich in the mineral zinc, which helps repair skin tissues (one fifth of the body's zinc content is found within the skin). This may be another reason why it is especially useful in caring for the fragile skin area around the eyes.

FENNEL *Foeniculum vulgare*

Fennel was named after the Latin word for hay, as it was thought to have the same scent as freshly mown hay. When Pliny the Elder wrote on the merits of herbs, he detailed twenty-two different curative effects of fennel. He had observed a snake rubbing its eyes on the plant and came to the conclusion that fennel was therefore good for the eyes. Two thousand years later, fennel is still associated with the eyes and an infusion made from the seeds is useful for making a compress to treat tired and sore eyes. Fennel is also reputed to be the herb of immortality and is associated with ageing well and longevity.

The main component of fennel oil is anethol, which is used to perfume toiletries such as shampoo and soap (see Essential Oils, page 51). Fennel tea also contains a small amount of the natural plant oils and is useful for expelling wind from the system, for cases of persistent hiccups and to pep up a weak digestive system. Fennel is commonly used to make gripe water, a childhood remedy for colic, and can help cases of flatulence and other intestinal disturbances. The essential oils contained in fennel have constituents similar to adrenalin, which may be why it has a tonic effect on the digestion and can stimulate the appetite. Fennel is traditionally an anti-nauseant and is often used to relieve morning sickness in pregnancy and motion sickness. It is also useful for relieving inflammations of mucous membranes such as the eyes and mouth, and is a time-honoured remedy for increasing milk production when breastfeeding.

GERANIUM *Pelargonium capitatum*

This well-known flowering plant is unusual because its scent is found mainly in the leaves and not in its attractive red and pink flowers. Depending upon the variety, geranium leaves may smell of peppermint, rose, orange, spices or even pineapple. All types are good to grow in the garden or in pots as they provide an attractive display of colour during the summer months and need almost no looking after.

Pelargonium capitatum is the variety most widely used in cosmetics as its leaves contain a rose scent, due to an alcohol called geraniol, which is also found in roses. Frequently used as a cheaper alternative to pure rose oil which has become prohibitively expensive (see also Essential Oils, page 52), this extract is gentle on the skin and can be used in moisturisers and skin lotions for dry and sensitive complexions. The roots of wild geranium *Geranium maculatum* are also used internally by medical herbalists for their astringent properties to treat diarrhoea and bowel diseases.

LAVENDER *Lavendula officinalis*

The word lavender was coined in the Middle Ages and comes from the Latin verb *lavare*, meaning to wash or clean. Lavender has been a popular herb in Britain for centuries and the use of this purple-flowered spiky plant dates back to the late sixteenth century. Lavender gets its distinctive smell from the small green pods that sit on either side of the small purple flowers. These pods contain the plant's essential oil, which has many medicinal properties. Medical herbalists may use lavender to treat irritability, stress and depression, and the oil can be used neat on the skin to help heal burns and wounds (see Essential Oils, page 54).

Lavender should be gathered in July or August, just before the flowers have fully opened, and spread out to dry in a warm place away from direct sunlight, which fades the flowers. When dry, the aromatic flower heads easily rub off between the fingers and thumb. These can be kept in a tightly sealed jar and used to make infusions or to fragrance pot-pourri.

MARIGOLD *Calendula officinalis*

Also known as pot marigold, this plant derives its botanical name from its flowers, which often bloom on the first day of the month, a time formerly known as the *calends*. In Anglo-Saxon days, marigolds were woven into garlands for feasts and weddings, as their golden colour symbolised strength and healing. The petals were also used to treat jaundice, headaches and sore, red eyes. The flower heads have distinctive orange petals which can be collected and used as a natural hair dye. The petals may also be scattered on to salads as an attractive garnish, and have a slightly bitter flavour.

One of the most useful skincare extracts is calendula oil, which is extracted from the petals by steeping them for a fortnight in pure vegetable oil, such as almond or olive oil. This contains natural steroid substances called sterols and is especially good for treating skin conditions like eczema, or cases where the skin has been damaged by steroid abuse.

A half-and-half mixture of calendula oil and St John's wort oil is an especially effective remedy for repairing scarred or damaged skin. This type of flower petal maceration also provides a rich source of beta carotene, a vitamin vitally important for healthy skin tissues. It is especially useful to boost the nutritional value of homemade moisturisers.

The juice from marigold petals can also be squeezed from the flower heads and used neat on spots and insect bits. Herbalists only use the petals of the marigold flower and favour the *officinalis* variety, which is available dried from herbal suppliers (this should not be confused with the many types of cultivated marigolds that are grown for the garden). Marigold tincture is also available and this can be mixed with equal parts of witch hazel to make a tonic for irritated, sensitive skins.

MINT *Mentha piperita*

Discovered by British botanist John Rea in 1700, this herb is named for its peppery smell. There are many varieties of mint including peppermint, spearmint and eau de cologne mint. The best to grow for beauty recipes is peppermint *Mentha piperita*. This variety has one of the strongest aromas and also works well in recipes for cooking. When planting mint in the garden it is advisable to place it in a bucket first before sinking it into the soil, otherwise its roots quickly spread and the plant takes over the entire garden.

Peppermint has many health and beauty benefits and it crops up in countless preparations. Peppermint oil contains many substances including turpentine and menthol, which give it a camphor-like smell. Cold on the skin, menthol is often included in refreshing skin tonics and invigorating shower foams. Traditionally used in toothpastes to refresh the mouth and teeth, menthol also numbs the gums and can relieve toothache. Peppermint has a good influence on the metabolism and peppermint tea is often drunk to improve the flow of bile to the liver, resulting in the correct digestion of fats. Being an astringent herb, peppermint tea is also useful in treating nausea and digestive upsets, and medical herbalists may use peppermint internally to relieve irritable bowel syndrome and dyspepsia.

Peppermint leaves have a bitter taste which means they contain elements that stimulate important digestive enzymes within the body. Recent research shows that oil of peppermint (which is contained to some degree in peppermint tea) can be used to treat irritable bowel syndrome and it is currently on trial in some hospitals (see also Essential Oils, page 56).

PRIMROSE *Primula vulgaris*

Primrose is another wild plant native to Britain that has excellent skincare properties. The primrose plant produces its flowers in early spring and so takes its name from the Latin *primus*, meaning first. The juice from the primrose leaves was used by herbalists for many years as an astringent skin tonic, and Culpeper commented that primrose ointment made from the leaves was an excellent salve for sore skins. In *Culpeper's Complete Herbal*, written in 1653, he urges, 'do not see your poor neighbour go with wounded limbs when a half-penny cost (for primrose salve) will heal them'. In herbalism, the roots and leaves of the primrose are the only parts that are used. These contain anti-inflammatory and anti-spasmodic extracts which used to be common cures for rheumatism, gout, insomnia and as a poultice to heal burns and wounds.

ROSE *Rosa damascena*

Called the Queen of Flowers, it is hard to beat the rose for its perfume and sheer beauty. Of the many varieties of roses grown in Britain it is the *Rosa damascena* that gives us some of the most wonderful scent. Originally from the Middle East, legend has it that this variety was born from a single drop of sweat falling from Mohammed's brow. It also gave its name to the town of Damascus in Syria, which was famed for damask silk woven in colours to match the flowers. One of the earliest records of the damask rose was by Greek historian Herodotus, who wrote that the flower had some sixty petals and a scent to surpass all others.

First used in perfumery, pure rose oil is frighteningly expensive as it takes around 110 kg (250 lb) of petals to produce a single ounce of concentrated essential oil. Still cultivated in a few areas such as Grasse in southern France, the rose petals must be picked by hand early in the morning before the sun rises high in the sky and evaporates the oil.

In addition to rose oil, rosewater is also a by-product of the distillation process that produces the essential oil (see page 57). This is a more common ingredient in skincare and a version can be made at home by steeping clean rose petals in water. Note that the rosewater commonly available from chemists is more frequently made with synthetic fragrance extracts, not roses. Genuine rosewater is available from herbal and aromatherapy suppliers and contains up to twenty per cent pure essential oils that are soluble in water and therefore left behind after the distillation process.

ROSEMARY *Rosmarinus officinalis*

Named from the Latin *ros marinus* which means dew of the sea, rosemary is rich in fragrant oils that the plant stores in cells, just beneath the leaf surface, visible only with a magnifier. These oils are released in the sunshine or a warm breeze or when the plant is handled (see Essential Oils, page 57). A simple rosemary oil maceration can be made by soaking a handful of clean, flowering stalks in a good quality almond or olive oil. Cover tightly and leave for at least a week before filtering the fragrant infusion. Use for rubbing into tired feet, or for adding to a refreshing bath. Rosemary has invigorating properties and has been used for centuries in beauty preparations, especially hair and scalp remedies. Naturally antiseptic, a rosemary hair rinse can be used to help dandruff and flakiness after the final shampoo.

Culpeper recommended rosemary 'to take away spots, marks and scars in the skin'. More recently, rosemary has been found to contain a substance called diosmin which helps strengthen fragile capillaries and may even improve disfiguring skin conditions such as broken thread veins. Rosemary tea is also recommended by modern herbalists to help ease migraine and headaches.

SAGE *Salvia officinalis*

Sage is a small shrubby herb with pale green leaves covered in downy hairs, which give them a greyish tinge. According to an Anglo Saxon manuscript, 'Why should man die when he can have sage?' and from this saying comes its botanical Latin name *salvia* meaning salvation. Sage has many unusual medicinal properties and is a powerful antiseptic (Chinese herbalists even use sage to boost brain power). Modern studies have shown that sage is a natural antibiotic and that it contains hormonal components similar to a vegetable form of oestrogen. For this reason a medical herbalist may use it when treating menstrual disorders, infertility or problems associated with the menopause. Sage tea is an excellent gargle for sore throats and is made by using one tablespoonful of leaves to each cup, infusing with boiling water for five minutes before straining and gargling (do not swallow). Sage oil is useful in a massage mixture rubbed into the neck to treat tonsillitis (see Essential Oils, page 58). Sage infusions made from the flowering tops of the plant are traditionally used to bring out the lustre of dark hair and can be added to the final rinse after shampooing.

ST JOHN'S WORT *Hypericum perforatum*

There are two anecdotes as to how this herb received its name. Some say it is named after St John the Baptist, as it usually flowers on his feast day of 24 June. Other herbal historians assert that it was called after the knights of the Crusades who hung it around their horses on St John's Eve to ward off evil spirits. Either way, this herb has attractive bright yellow flowers with a cluster of fine stamens. Its small green leaves are dotted with oil glands containing caproic acid which gives off a pungent smell that has been unkindly likened to wet goat's fur. When the leaves are held up to the light they are seen to be full of tiny holes, which is why the French call this herb *mille-pertuis*, or a thousand perforations. Historically, St John's wort is one of our most useful herbs for health and beauty as it has more medicinal properties than almost any other plant. When prescribed for internal use by a medical herbalist, St John's wort can treat a range of emotional problems, including anxiety, depression and long-term stress. It is widely used in Europe as a natural alternative to synthetic sleeping pills and tranquillizers. Scientific interest in this unusual herb has increased in recent years with evidence that the oil has not only a mood-boosting substance but is also an anti-viral agent. This may be due to a compound called hypericin found within the herb. Externally, the herb has astringent, antiseptic properties and is a mild painkiller. As the plant's flowers also contain oil glands, its petals may be macerated or infused in pure vegetable oil to produce an attractive pink oil. This oil contains relatively high concentrations of flavonoids, tannins and carotenoids (useful skin nutrients). This valuable natural healer can be used on the skin to hasten wound healing and to reduce scarring from burns. It is an excellent addition to any first-aid box and is useful in skincare remedies for sensitive complexions.

STINGING NETTLE *Urtica dioica*

Usually considered to be an unwelcome weed, the stinging nettle has many uses in herbalism. The entire stem and leaves of the plant are covered with tiny stiff hairs which contain formic acid. This is released on to the skin as soon as the plant is touched and causes an allergic reaction. Despite the hazards of their cultivation, stinging nettles can be cooked and eaten just like any other herb. They are best harvested in the spring when the shoots are young and tender. These can be lightly boiled and served like spinach or spring greens (one of Prince Charles's favourite dishes is said to be nettle soup). Rich in vitamin C and iron, nettles are one of the best sources of chlorophyll, the plant pigment which is similar in structure to the haemoglobin in red blood cells.

Stinging nettles also have diuretic properties and capsules are often prescribed by medical herbalists for a variety of disorders including anaemia, water retention and gout. They may also use nettles to treat skin problems, such as childhood and allergic eczema, as well as cases of poor circulation. Stinging nettles contain the trace minerals silica and potassium which strengthen the skin, and are used for many skin conditions.

Added to skin fresheners, nettles can be used to make a beneficial facial wash with mildly astringent properties. Nettle infusions are also useful as a hair tonic as they add sheen to all hair types and are widely reputed to prevent hair loss.

SWEET MARJORAM *Origanum marjorana*

A common culinary herb with tiny white or pink flowers, sweet marjoram is also traditionally used in haircare treatments such as shampoos and scalp lotions. Sweet marjoram has an attractive herby smell that is often used in perfumery, espe-cially for men's aftershave. The oil is extracted from the plant's leaves and young shoots and has antiseptic and antiviral properties (see Essential Oils, page 58).

THYME *Thymus vulgaris*

Thyme is a hardy herb that survives in poor soils and dry climates. Thyme leaves contain a strong antiseptic substance called thymol, which is use-ful in several health and beauty remedies. Thyme oil is used in soaps and added to some skincare preparations for its antibacterial properties. The oil is also useful for treating sore throats and a few drops may be mixed with almond oil and rubbed on to the neck to treat tonsillitis or inflamed glands. An infusion of thyme leaves also makes a good anti-dandruff scalp tonic (see Essential Oils, page 59). Medical herbalists may use thyme to treat a variety of disorders, includ-ing respiratory problems, as it acts as a deconges-tant and expectorant. It has also been used to treat menstrual disorders and mouth infections. Although the chief constituent of thyme oil is thymol it also contains borneol and linalol, which give it a pleasanter smell. Not all creatures find the scent attractive though, and sachets of dried thyme mixed with lavender and placed amongst clothes are a useful way of deterring insects and fabric-eating moths.

VIOLET *Viola odorata*

The violet is well known for its sweet, heady fragrance, which sadly fades as soon as the flowers are picked. This is due to its chemical composition which contains the volatile substance ionine, from which the name violet is derived. Violet herbal extracts have anti-inflammatory properties and are useful as a skin soother. A diluted version can also be used as a mouthwash for throat and mouth infections. Medical herbalists may use extracts from the flowers and leaves internally, as a powerful expectorant to treat respiratory and lung disorders.

WITCH HAZEL *Hamamelis virginiana*

Historically used to prevent internal bleeding, witch hazel extract is a useful astringent that also soothes the skin. It is one of the most widely used plants in Western medicine and the leaves contain high levels of a tannin, hamamelitannin, which gives them astringent properties and a healing action on veins. Tannins occur widely in nature and are used to heal the skin. They are responsible for binding protein in the skin to form a tight layer which is resistant to disease. This separates the bacteria which have settled on the skin and protects against potential irritation.

Witch hazel lotion is made from the leaves and twigs of the plant and is available from most chemists. Although this contains only ten per cent tannins and up to fifteen per cent alcohol, it is a handy ingredient for homemade skin fresheners, especially for inflamed skin conditions, compresses to heal wounds and soothing face masks.

Witch hazel capsules are also prescribed for internal use by medical herbalists to treat problems with veins and capillaries, including varicose veins, piles and broken thread veins on the face. Compresses made from witch hazel are also an effective external remedy for haemorrhoids (piles) and other cases of swelling.

YARROW *Achillea millefolium*

A tall herb with attractive feathery foliage and white flowers, yarrow gets its name from the Latin for 'thousand-leaf'. It is traditionally held that Aphrodite persuaded Achilles to dress his wounds with yarrow at the siege of Troy and it has since been associated with love and loyalty, especially for those injured in battle. Yarrow has been used by generations of wounded soldiers up until the Great War. It is well-known as a healing herb and even helps other plants nearby resist attacks from disease and pests.

Yarrow has astringent properties and is useful for pepping up a poor circulation and for improving skin tone. It also contains azulenes, the skin soothers found in some other herbs, notably chamomile. Culpeper used yarrow to prevent hair loss and modern herbalists regard yarrow as a useful all-round tonic that can also help to lower blood pressure. Externally, an infusion of yarrow leaves and flowers can be used as an effective skin tonic, and is useful for soothing sore skin conditions. It is also efficient at promoting wound healing and improving the skin's own micro-circulation.

ESSENTIAL OILS

In addition to plant extracts made from flowers, leaves and roots, many botanicals also contain essential oils which are remarkably effective in beauty recipes. Essential oils can be defined in two ways: their scientific explanation is that many plants contain high concentrations of volatile oils which give plants their distinctive flavours and aromas. These aromatic, essential or volatile oils are made up from a wide variety of different chemical constituents. A single essential oil may contain as many as fifty individual ingredients, including substances such as phenol, carvacrol, linalol and geraniol.

Aromatherapists, who use essential oils for therapeutic massage, are more likely to adopt a less clinical approach when it comes to defining essential oils. They often describe them as the 'life force' or 'soul' of the plant and believe that each essential oil has different characteristics and uses. Whether you take the more pragmatic and analytical approach, or prefer to follow the folklore, there is no doubt that essential oils can be extremely useful in caring for the body and encouraging well-being.

Essential oils can be extracted from plants in two main ways — by using either steam or solvent distillation. Steam distillation involves placing the plant material in a flask, heating to a high temperature and collecting the steam. As the steam cools and turns back into water, the essential oil from the plant floats to the surface where it can be collected. Steam distillation is the best method for extracting pure essential oils and most of the expensive varieties are extracted this way. The other method of solvent extraction is faster and involves placing the plant material in a flask and mixing with a chemical solvent such as hexane. The mixture is stirred and heated to release the essential oils from the plant before the solvent is evaporated away. Solvent extraction is common in the perfume industry, where natural flower fragrances are still used by some of the more expensive scents. However, it is not the best method for producing essential oils for skincare as traces of the solvent are invariably left behind in the oil.

Technically, anything that has been produced by solvent extraction should be called an 'absolute' and not an 'essential' oil. Common examples of these include rose absolute or jasmine absolute, which are extremely rare to find as essential oils made by steam distillation.

The main problem when buying essential oils is knowing exactly what is inside the bottle. Always look for the words 'pure essential oil', on the label which mean that the oil has not been diluted with a cheaper vegetable oil before bottling. Some oils are sold as 'aromatherapy oils' or 'fragrance oils' and should not be confused with genuine, highly concentrated essential oils.

Most healthfood shops stock reputable ranges and there is also a list of reliable mail-order suppliers at the back of the book. Another safety check is to make sure that your supplier is registered with EOTA (the Essential Oil Trade Association) as their members are regularly checked for quality control. If in doubt, go by the price. Essential oils are not cheap and in most cases you do get what you pay for.

However, because they are only used in tiny amounts, a good-quality essential oil will last a long time if kept cool and dark, and most oils have many health and beauty uses. All essential oils are naturally antiseptic and many are also naturally antibiotic. Some even help to boost the immune system and fight off bacterial, viral and fungal infections.

Aromatherapy

Aromatherapy is the art of using these essential oils mixed in a base or 'carrier' oil, such as almond or grapeseed oil, combined with massage. Aromatherapy works by releasing the aroma of these oils into the atmosphere where they are taken up by the nerve endings in the nose and relayed to the brain. Here they can have a powerful effect on mood, emotions and mental state. Essential or volatile oils also have a very small molecular structure enabling them to slip through the surface of the skin and end up in the bloodstream. This is why the oils used on the skin in massage can be so effective in treating not only skin complaints but also disorders as diverse as hormonal problems and cellulite.

Because essential oils end up circulating in the bloodstream, it is wise to use caution if using them during pregnancy. Stimulating herb and spice oils should be avoided and replaced with gentler oils such as chamomile, sandalwood, geranium and lemon (see below). While small amounts of almost any oil are quite safe, for regular use it is best to consult a professional aromatherapist for personal advice during pregnancy.

Pregnant or not, all essential oils are highly concentrated and should only ever be used in small quantities and always diluted either in a carrier oil or cream, or diffused in a warm bath. The only exceptions to this rule are when using lavender oil neat on burns, or dabbing small amounts of tea tree oil on to spots and pimples.

Essential oils to avoid during pregnancy

Aniseed, bay, basil, cassia, clary sage, cedarwood, clove, coriander, cinnamon, cypress, eucalyptus, hyssop, juniper, lemongrass, nutmeg, sage, savory, thyme, marjoram (including sweet marjoram), myrrh, pennyroyal, pine, rosemary, sage, tansy, tea tree, wintergreen and wormwood.

Essential oils recommended by many aromatherapists during pregnancy

Citrus oils (e.g. mandarin, tangerine, bergamot and lemon), sandalwood, neroli, jasmine, geranium and chamomile. After the first three months, lavender, rose and melissa may also be used in moderation.

Essential oils for beauty

The best essential oils for beauty recipes are listed in alphabetical order below.

BERGAMOT *Citrus bergamia*

The bergamot is a cross between an orange and a lemon and grows in northern Italy around the area of Bergamo, not far from Milan, which gave the fruit its name. The essential oil is extracted from the oil-bearing glands on the surface of the fruit. It has a sweet, citrus smell and is used to flavour Earl Grey tea and is a traditional ingredient in eau de cologne. The uplifting, refreshing scent of bergamot oil is useful for adding to a reviving bath and is the perfect solution for lifting the spirits after a tiring day. Bergamot suits combination and oily skin types but as with all citrus oils, should not be used in the sun or before going on a sunbed. This is because they contain substances that can photo-sensitise the skin in strong sunlight and may cause allergies.

CHAMOMILE *Chamomilla matricara*

This essential oil comes from the flowers of this European herb. There are two main types of chamomile essential oil, Roman chamomile and German chamomile, and both are useful in skincare. However, it is the German variety *Chamomilla matricara* that is highly prized and more expensive.

Chamomile oil has soothing, relaxing and calming properties and is safe to use on small children and during pregnancy. Both types of oil suit dry, sensitive and easily irritated skins and it is one of the few that can be used on inflamed skin conditions such as eczema.

CYPRESS *supressus sempervirens*

This essential oil is extracted from the leaves and twigs of the evergreen cypress tree. Its smell is similar to pine, although slightly sweeter and less overpowering. It is a useful oil in body care as it stimulates the circulation and can be used to treat water retention. Cypress is often added to anti-

cellulite remedies and is excellent for improving over-all skin tone. It is mildly astringent and is best suited to normal, combination and oily skin types. Cypress oil can also be added to a warm bath to stimulate and revive aching muscles after strenuous exercise.

EUCALYPTUS *Eucalyptus globulus*

Native to Australia where eucalyptus shoots are the favourite food of koala bears, the essential oil comes from the leaves and twigs of this tall tree. Eucalyptus is a powerful and unmistakably pungent oil widely used in cough mixtures and bronchial expectorants. The essential oil is naturally antibiotic and anti-inflammatory and therefore has a wide range of medicinal uses. In skincare it is excellent for healing spots, boils and pimples and may be dabbed neat in tiny quantities on to the affected area.

Eucalyptus oil is also useful as a burning essence to ease the stuffiness of nasal congestion. Two or three drops in a bowl of hot water also makes an instant invigorating steam inhalation. Eucalyptus oil has high levels of camphor, which is an irritant, and is therefore unsuitable for use on the skin of babies and children under the age of two. It is also too strong to use in most facial recipes but one drop mixed with a dessertspoonful of jojoba oil is a useful antiseptic massage oil for spotty backs and complexions.

FENNEL *Foeniculum vulgare*

The seeds of the fennel flower are crushed to produce this essential oil, which is a useful diuretic and good for cases of water retention. Only the essential oil known as 'sweet fennel' should be used on the body and this is traditionally associated with female reproductive organs.

Although fennel oil is best avoided during pregnancy, a few drops mixed with almond oil are often helpful for massage during breastfeeding as it can help to increase the milk supply. Sweet fennel has a mild aniseed scent and is often included in skin care to tone puffy and slackened tissues.

FRANKINCENSE *Boswellia carterii*

This essential oil dates back to biblical times and beyond, when it was burned as incense in temples. The oil comes from the gummy resin produced by a tree that is native to Somalia in Africa. Frankincense has a purifying and toning action on the skin and is especially useful in anti-wrinkle remedies. Used sparingly, it can be added to night creams and neck lotions to help deter fine lines and wrinkles by stimulating skin cells.

Perhaps because of its association with churches, the aroma of frankincense also has a calming effect when inhaled and is a useful burning oil for times when we are under pressure or if we need greater mental concentration. Massaging a few drops into the temples and scalp is also a quick and easy way to clear the mind and reduce tension headaches.

GERANIUM *Pelargonium graveolens*

Also referred to as *Geranium rosata* because of its rosy aroma, this essential oil affords a fabulous aroma to many skincare preparations and is most commonly produced in Morocco and Egypt. The essential oil is extracted from the leaves and flowers and, like most floral oils, is safe for use during pregnancy and for children.

Aromatherapists have several uses for geranium oil in addition to its skincare benefits. It has been found to act as a nerve tonic and may have a stimulatory effect on the adrenal cortex that could actually stimulate the production of corticosteroid hormones. These hormones suppress the inflammatory response and depress the immune processes. Although clinical studies have yet to be carried out, some aromatherapists are using geranium oil to treat MS.

In all, there are several hundred varieties of geranium but only a few are used to make the sweet smelling essential oils. Among the best is rose geranium, which is extracted from a variety of geranium leaves that smell just like roses, and this is an exceptionally good oil for adding to skincare recipes. It is also a good option for adding a rose fragrance to recipes at a fraction of the cost of pure rose oil. All geranium essential oils have a toning and smoothing action on the skin and suit most skin types, including dry and sensitive complexions. They also have a normalising action on the skin and are good for balancing a combination complexion and for combatting cellulite. In addition to rose geranium, there are other types of geranium oils that may be used in recipes which have a variety of sweet, floral fragrances. However, all should be used sparingly as it is easy to overdo the amount needed and end up with a sickly sweet scent

GINGER *Zingiber officinale*

This essential oil is extracted from the roots or rhizome of this traditional Chinese herb. Used for thousands of years to ward off coughs, colds and general infections, ginger oil is a powerful antiseptic and has a warming action on the body. It should be used with caution in skincare as it is extremely potent and can easily irritate sensitive complexions. However, ginger oil is useful for boosting the blood supply to the surface of the skin and can help complaints such as chilblains, rheumatism and muscular aches and pains. It is also a perfect ingredient for making warming footbaths, especially if you are suffering from a cold or influenza.

JASMINE *Jasminum officinale*

Pure jasmine essential oil from Grasse in the South of France is one of the most expensive natural skincare ingredients. It comes from the tiny white flowers which must be picked by hand each morning before the sun rises high in the sky and evaporates their oil content. The scent of the jasmine flowers is so strong that it fills the hillsides in Grasse during the traditional harvest months of September and October. Once the flowers have been collected, the oil is extracted using solvents to make a jasmine absolute (steam-distilled jasmine oil is extremely rare). The smell of jasmine is extremely sweet and over-powering if used in excess. It is a costly ingredient, but a little goes a very long way and one small bottle will last several years if stored in a cool, dark place. Jasmine oil is traditionally associated with femininity and has uplifting properties. One drop will luxuriously fragrance a warm bath and leave a lingering aroma on the skin. Jasmine oil suits all skin types, especially delicate skins, and is reputed to improve the appearance of stretchmarks and scar tissue.

JUNIPER BERRY *Juniperus communis*

This essential oil comes from the dark, ripe berries of the prickly juniper bush that grows wild throughout Southern Europe. The oil has a distinctively pungent and slightly bitter aroma that is used by distillers to flavour gin. It is also used in perfumery and often added to macho-smelling aftershaves for men. Juniper essential oil has anti-fungal properties and is also a powerful diuretic. This is why it is often added to lotions and oils that help treat cellulite, and puffiness due to fluid retention. However, it has a powerful effect on the skin and should be used sparingly. In skincare, juniper oil suits combination and oily skin types and can be used in facial oils to treat acne.

LAVENDER *Lavendula officinalis*

This is the king of essential oils and an essential part of all health and beauty routines. It is extracted from the flowering spikes of the lavender plant and there are many different varieties. The best is from *Lavendula officinalis* and this, of course, is also the most expensive. Spike lavender, or *Lavendula spica*, is another variety that is also popular with aromatherapists. By crossing these two varieties of lavender, botanists have produced a similar plant called lavendin. This hybrid plant

is much easier to grow and produces many more flowering spikes and so its essential oil is quite a bit cheaper than pure lavender oil. As an example, lavender produces around 15-20 kilos of essential oil per hectare, while lavendin produces between 8-120 kilos per hectare. Not surprisingly, there is a temptation for less scrupulous suppliers to sell lavendin incorrectly labelled as the more expensive pure lavender oil. However, lavendin does have a lovely smell and is widely used in the perfume industry and by toiletry manufacturers to disguise the smell of harsh detergents.

Pure, neat lavender oil can be used on burns (worth keeping some in the kitchen) and rapidly heals scar tissues. It is also used to treat headaches, including migraine, stress and insomnia. It is gentler on the skin and more effective at healing open wounds than modern antiseptics and is definitely an essential oil for the first-aid box. My husband used to be sceptical of the powers of essential oils until he witnessed the speed at which lavender healed his burnt hand. Now, he'll bitterly complain if he can't find his first-aid bottle! Lavender oil also has many other uses and is a versatile ingredient in many skincare recipes. It has fortifying, balancing and toning properties, as well as being naturally antibiotic and anti-fungal. It suits most skin types except very dry, sensitive complexions and is an excellent oil for the bath and general massage blends.

LEMON *Citrus limonum*

This essential oil is one of the easiest to extract as it comes from the oil-laden glands on the fruit's skin. This means it is also one of the cheapest essential oils to buy. Lemon oil has many useful skincare properties as it is anti-fungal, diuretic and naturally stimulating. However, it should not be used directly on the skin before going out into the sunshine as it contains ingre-

dients that can react with ultra-violet light and cause skin sensitivity.

Lemon oil is useful for adding to baths to pep up the circulation and revive the senses. It acts as an all-round tonic and is helpful for adding to skin fresheners, anti-cellulite creams and lotions for combination or oily skin types.

MANDARIN *Citrus nobilis*

This is another essential oil that is easily extracted from the rind of a citrus fruit. It has a sweet, subtle scent and is good for adding to children's baths and skincare routines. Mandarin oil is soothing, uplifting and toning. It also helps improve the circulation and so is a good ingredient for many body oils and lotions. A few drops of mandarin oil also makes a reviving bath and it is useful for cases of insomnia and nervous tension. As with other citrus oils, it should not be used before exposing the skin to sunlight or before going on a sunbed. All citrus oils also have a limited shelf-life and should be used within one year of purchase.

MELISSA *Melissa officinalis*

True melissa is extremely rare but it can be found – at a price! It is extracted from lemon balm leaves and has a powerful lemony fragrance (one or two drops added to a warm bath will not only fragrance the water but also the entire home). Most essential oil sold as melissa oil is more likely to be an inferior blend of citrus oils and lemongrass. Look for the Latin words *Melissa officinalis* on the label, or go by the price. As with most essential oils from reputable suppliers, you tend to get what you pay for.

Melissa oil was an important ingredient in the famous Melissa Water, one of the first commercial perfumes made in medieval times by Carmelite monks in Italy. It has soothing, uplifting and toning properties and is one of the very best oils for adding to a reviving bath or massage oil blend. It suits all skin types and adds a wonderfully fresh scent to lotions for the face and body.

NEROLI *Citrus autantium*

This sweet-smelling oil comes from orange blossom and is a traditional skincare ingredient. It is also probably the most expensive essential oil you can buy. Neroli oil has a fabulously soft, fruit scent that is widely used in eau de cologne and general perfumery (it takes its name from an Italian princess who used neroli as her favourite perfume). The essential oil has uplifting and restorative properties and can help ease tension and relax the body. It also helps improve the skin's own micro-circulation and can help problem, spotty skins. Several aromatherapists are also on record as saying that neroli has a stimulating effect on fresh, young skin cells. Neroli is best suited to normal, combination and oily skin types, although it can also be used for its fabulous fragrance alone in many beauty remedies.

PATCHOULI *Pogostemon patchouli*

An aromatic, distinctive oil that comes from the dried leaves of a Chinese herb, patchouli oil has been used as a natural perfume for thousands of years, especially in the Middle East and India, where it was regarded as a sacred herb. The essential oil has many skincare properties and is both antibiotic and antifungal. In addition, it has a toning, strengthening effect on the skin and can be diluted with wheatgerm oil and used to repair damaged skin and fade scar tissue.

PEPPERMINT *Mentha piperata*

The leaves, flowers and stalks of this common garden herb are used to make peppermint essential oil. Because of its naturally high menthol content, peppermint feels cool and refreshing on the skin and is effective in invigorating skincare products such as foot lotion and after-sun creams. It may be added to baths to tone and stimulate the skin, but do not use more than a couple of drops otherwise it will make even the hottest bathwater feel cold against the skin. Peppermint is also useful for clearing the mind and encouraging productivity (the Japanese squirt it into the atmosphere in their factories as it has been proved to enhance output). Due to its high menthol content, peppermint oil is a common irritant and is not suitable for use on the skin of babies or children under two years of age. It should also be avoided by those with delicate or more sensitive skins and is best suited to oilier complexions.

PINE *Pinus palustris*

This powerful antiseptic oil has many medicinal uses and is widely used in disinfectants and detergents. The essential oil is extracted from the needles and twigs of the American pine tree and has a pungent, distinctive smell. Pine oil is often too overpowering to use in beauty remedies, although it is useful for some scalp oils and as a topical antiseptic for spots and boils. It is a potent stimulant and a couple of drops in a warm bath will rev up the circulation and get the body glowing. Pine oil also helps to fight off infections and is a useful oil in steam inhalations.

RAVENSARA *Ravensara aromatica*

This unusual essential oil is produced from the leaves of a Madagascan shrub. It is a rare oil not currently found in the high street and may need to be tracked down from a professional essential oil supplier. Ravensara is a gently antiseptic essential oil with strong anti-viral properties. It has been used to treat conditions as diverse as pimples to plague, and is a useful ingredient for the treatment of inflamed skin conditions, including acne and minor blemishes. Professional therapists may use ravensara to combat infections and also to help treat muscular pains. The neat essential oil has an aroma similar to cloves (it should not be confused with clove bud oil) and can be dabbed on to a handkerchief and sniffed to help banish a cold.

ROSE *Rosa damascena*

As with jasmine oil, pure rose oil is rare and extremely expensive. Most pure rose oil is, in fact, a rose absolute produced by solvent extraction. It is extremely difficult for chemists to copy the natural rose fragrance synthetically as it has over 500 different chemical constituents. To the majority of perfumiers, Bulgarian rose oil is the only variety to use; however, this is scarce. Purists claim that the oil from Turkish roses is closest to the prized Bulgarian rose oil, as it produced from plants originally shipped from Bulgaria.

Rose oil has fabulous skincare properties which is why it has been so highly prized throughout the centuries. It is traditionally associated with formulations for dry, irritated or inflamed skin conditions. Some claim it can even help prevent wrinkles and reduce broken thread veins within the skin. One useful by-product of essential rose oil distillation is rosewater. However, pure rosewater is as rare as pure rose oil, so check its origins before you buy.

ROSEMARY *Rosmarinus officinalis*

The flowering tops of this herb are used to extract the strongly scented essential oil. One of the most antiseptic and stimulating oils, rosemary also has diuretic properties. It also has a high camphor content and should not be used on babies or small children. Rosemary essential oil contains useful quantities of the bioflavonoid diosmin. This has been shown in French studies to stimulate the skin's circulation and is currently being studied for use in the treatment of varicose veins and leg ulcers.

It suits combination and problem skins and can also be used in treatments to improve the condition of cellulite and loss of skin tone.

ROSEWOOD *Aniba rosaeodora*

Also known as *rose de bois*, this essential oil smells like rose petals although it actually comes from the bark of a South American tree. Although rosewood has fewer skincare properties than pure rose oil, it is toning on the skin and has an uplifting scent that can be used as a subtle fragrance in skin creams. It is also useful in body massage blends and for adding to a warm, reviving bath.

Regrettably, rosewood trees are being destroyed at an alarming rate in South America. As they take forty odd years to grow before the oil can be extracted, there will soon be a severe shortage of rosewood essential oil. Ho wood and Ho wood leaf oils are a possible alternative, as they contain an almost identical linalol content and a similarly sweet, floral-woody scent. Sustained Ho wood plantations are managed in the Far East, where the young trees are cut back to the stump and stripped of their leaves every two years. This could become a very useful source of essential oil production for the future. Alternatively, leading British aromatherapist Shirley Price suggests making a rosewood-scented blend by combining geranium or palmarosa with a touch of sandalwood essential oils.

SAGE *Salvia officinalis*

This powerful essential oil should be used with caution and not at all during pregnancy. It is highly stimulating and antiseptic, and has many medicinal uses. It is best suited to problem skins that benefit from its antibacterial properties and it also helps dandruff and flaking scalps.

SANDALWOOD *Santalum album*

Made from the wood chippings of the sandalwood tree which is native to India, this essential oil has a distinctive, spicy aroma. It has a high alcohol content, making it highly antiseptic, and its aroma is also reputed to be an aphrodisiac. Sandalwood oil is a useful ingredient in many skincare remedies as it has a soothing and strengthening action on the skin. It is one of the gentlest oils to use in facial massage and can help soothe irritated and inflamed skin conditions. Sandalwood oil suits all skin types and can even be used in treatments to help problem complexions including acne. It is an important skincare oil and has potentially powerful anti-ageing properties in skin creams. Pure sandalwood essential oil has been found to stimulate fibroblast cell growth within the deepest levels of the skin. This in turn could lead to an increase in surface skin cell turnover and a fresher, younger-looking complexion. A few drops added to a warm bath will transform it into a refreshing pick-me-up treatment and the oil also adds a subtle aroma to massage blends and natural perfumes.

SWEET MARJORAM *Origanum marjorana*

This essential oil is made from the flowering tops and leaves of the herb. There are several different types of marjoram and the closely related oregano oil, but only sweet marjoram should be used in skincare. Unfortunately, many of the cheaper essential oils on offer contain oregano or Spanish marjoram, which are far harsher on the skin. If in doubt, check that the oil is either *Origanum marjorana* or *Origanum hortensis*. It is strongly antiseptic and has calming, sedating properties that make it suitable for treating stress and insomnia (a few drops in a warm bedtime bath helps to relax the body and promote a good night's sleep).

Sweet marjoram is also useful in massage blends designed to help sports injuries, muscular aches and sprains. Used in skincare, sweet marjoram suits oily and combination skin types and is useful for dabbing neat on to spots and pimples.

TEA TREE *Melaleuca alternifolia*

This increasingly popular oil comes from the leaves and twigs of an Australian tree. It has powerful antiseptic and anti-fungal properties, and is also anti-viral and naturally antibiotic, making it one of the most useful medicinal essential oils. It can be used to treat fungal infections such as candidiasis (thrush) and is several times more effective at killing germs than household disinfectant. First used by the Aborigines thousands of year ago, tea tree oil was issued in the first-aid kits of Australian soldiers in the Second World War. More recent trials by skin doctors have also shown that tea tree oil is effective at treating spotty, acne-prone skin and can be more helpful than many shop-bought preparations. For example, it is better at treating acne than benzoyl peroxide and yet has fewer skin-damaging side effects. Tea tree oil is best suited to oily and problem skins and may also be applied neat in small quantities to clear up spots and pimples. The essential oil is also useful for improving scalp disorders such as dandruff and a few drops may be added to shampoos and scalp lotions.

THYME *Thymus vulgaris*

This is another highly medicinal essential oil that has been used for centuries for its powerfully antiseptic properties. It is made from the flowering tips of this common herb and has anti-viral and anti-fungal actions on the skin. A powerful healer, thyme oil must be used with caution and care on the skin. It is best suited to massage blends for sports injuries, arthritis and circulatory problems. It is useful in small doses to invigorate aching limbs and aromatherapists may also use the oil to help cases of high blood pressure or menstrual irregularity.

Personally, I use sweet thyme essential oil as a strong anti-bacterial lotion, dabbing very small amounts on to the neck to soothe the inflammation and pain of tonsillitis or other throat infections. It is also useful used in tiny quantities on swollen glands to prevent 'flu bugs from taking hold.

YLANG YLANG *Canang odorat*

The bright yellow flowers from a Madagascan tree produce this exotic essential oil which has a sweet smell that can be used as a cheaper alternative to jasmine oil. Ylang ylang has invigorating, uplifting properties and is best suited to normal and combination skin types (it can occasionally irritate sensitive skins). The essential oil is also reputed to have an aphrodisiac effect and is certainly useful as a general tonic in times of stress. It can be used in skincare to add a subtle fragrance to many recipes and is also an excellent addition to reviving massage blends.

FRUITS AND VEGETABLES

Most everyday fruits and vegetables make excellent ingredients for skincare. This is because they contain valuable enzymes that digest surface bacteria and leave the complexion glowing with health. Enzymes are completely destroyed by any kind of heat treatment, which is why most commercial skincare products cannot contain them. Freshly-made fruit and vegetable face masks are the best ways to put these naturally healing agents to use. For best results, make sure the fruits or vegetables are as fresh as possible and free from dust and dirt. It is also worth choosing organically grown varieties where possible, as these do not contain traces of chemical pesticides, herbicides or fungicides that have no place on our plates, let alone our face.

Apple

There are over 1000 different varieties of apples and all are good sources of vitamin C and the vegetable form of vitamin A, beta-carotene. Apples also contain minerals needed by the skin, including traces of potassium, calcium and magnesium. In addition, apples are a rich source of certain fruit acids, notably malic and tartaric acid which help to slough off dead cells from the skin's surface. They are useful ingredients in face masks and pure apple juice is an effective toner for oily and combination complexions.

Avocado

The avocado is one of nature's best beautifiers and contains all the ingredients needed to keep our skin cells healthy. It is naturally rich in plant oils that contain essential fatty acids to moisturise and smooth the skin. The avocado also contains potassium, B vitamins, beta-carotene, vitamin E and traces of iron.

Avocados can be used on their own to make a moisturising face mask or added to hair conditioners and skin scrubs. The insides of the avocado skin are also good to rub over the body just before a shower as this dislodges dead skin cells and leaves the body feeling smooth.

Banana

The banana is nature's own convenience food and contains reasonable levels of vitamins and minerals including potassium, magnesium and phosphorus, as well as traces of beta-carotene, folic acid and vitamin C. The sticky texture of mashed bananas also has many uses in natural beauty. Banana paste can be used as a skin-soothing face mask and also makes an excellent conditioning hair pack for dry, brittle hair.

Carrot

This root vegetable are extraordinarily rich in beta-carotene (hence the name carrot), the skin-saving nutrient that gives so many fruits and vegetables a vivid colour. The main benefit of beta-carotene is as an antioxidant, which means that it protects the skin from damage caused by free radical activity. This is a highly destructive process which occurs when particles of oxygen trigger a chain reaction of cell damage within the body.

The best way to use carrots in skincare is to soak grated carrot in a good quality vegetable oil for a few days. The oil may then be strained off and used as a basic massage oil or added to other skincare blends. Take care when using carrot oil though, because if the colour of the liquid is too dark, it can temporarily stain the skin orange. Always use organically grown carrots as conventional carrot crops tend to contain unacceptably high levels of poisonous pesticides including diazaphos and triazophos, which are harmful to health and skin.

Cucumber

Popular with the Ancient Greeks for its soothing and refreshing properties, a strip or two of fresh cucumber placed over the eyes reduces puffiness and swelling. According to the seventeenth-century herbalist Culpeper, cucumber makes a good face wash for cleansing the skin and clearing the eyes. Although cucumber is mainly water it does contain traces of useful nutrients, including vitamin C, potassium, silicon and sulphur.

Lemon

All citrus fruits are naturally rich in vitamin C, which is required by the skin to make collagen. This is a type of protein that literally holds the skin together, and maintains flexibility and strength. Lemon rind is also full of natural essential oils and if you peel a lemon with your fingers you will see the tiny oil glands on the surface of the fruit burst open to release the fragrant oils. Lemon rind can be added to a warm bath to invigorate the body, but make sure the lemons are the unwaxed variety which have not been coated with chemical fungicides. Lemon juice is also useful as a mild form of natural acid, which helps soften hard water and dislodge detergent and soap residues from the skin.

Papaya

Also known as the paw-paw, papaya is a useful skincare ingredient because it contains the enzyme papain. This is a powerful fruit enzyme that digests protein and can be used on the skin to get rid of dead skin cells that can clog the pores and lead to spots. Papain has also been used by herbalists to help heal scar tissue and assist wound healing. The inside of papaya skins can be rubbed over the body before stepping into the shower and this is also a gentle way to shift dead skin cells that tend to accumulate on the upper arms, elbows, hips and thighs.

Pineapple

The pineapple contains another potent protein-digesting enzyme called bromalin which is also an excellent skin buffer. In Sri Lanka, women rub the insides of pineapples over their bodies to remove dead skin cells, and pineapple skin can also be used as the basis for a facial scrub. Fresh pineapple is the best type to use in skincare as the tinned variety has been heat treated and this destroys some of its natural enzymes. Pineapple is an excellent ingredient in face masks and treatments for spotty, problem complexions as it gently dissolves sebum and keeps the pores free from dirt and dead cell debris. However, it should be avoided by those with sensitive skins and not used around the eyes or lips.

Natural skin science

During the last thirty years there have been many technological advances in skincare and today's beauty products are sophisticated formulas containing a combination of synthetically derived ingredients and natural extracts. In fact, it's rare these days, particularly at the expensive end of the market, to see a new skincare product that doesn't contain 'special' ingredients with scientific names such as ceramides and liposomes.

We live in hope of a cream that can smooth our wrinkles, reduce skin damage and protect our skin against pollution and environmental factors and it is all too easy to be taken in by promising claims if we don't understand the technology.

Despite the scientific developments in skincare, the emphasis on natural beauty has never been stronger and virtually every major skincare range contains some herbal extracts, essential oils, vitamins and minerals. One of the many benefits of natural skincare ingredients, such as the herbs echinacea and aloe vera, is the wealth of scientific literature, folklore and anecdotal information on their skin benefits. The majority of natural ingredients have been tried and tested for centuries and their anti-inflammatory, antiseptic, wound healing, skin protecting and moisturising properties have been well documented. In contrast, we know very little about some of the new breed of skincare ingredients and their long-term effects.

Many skincare ingredients perform very specific tasks. For example, there are binders to maintain the product's consistency, colours for dyeing it, emulsifiers to hold liquids together, fragrances and fixatives to prevent the odour vapourising. Other ingredients act as humectants to keep the product moist, preservatives prevent it from spoiling, while thickeners add body. The chemistry of modern skincare products may be baffling, but many of these special ingredients have their origins in nature, for example, vitamin E is a natural preserver while sorbitol is a natural humectant that comes from berries.

Below is an A to Z of some of the ingredients that are commonly used in skincare and anti-ageing products, highlighting what they can – and can't – do for your skin.

Alpha-Hydroxy Acids (AHAs)

These are natural acids found in fruit, vegetables and protein sources such as milk. The most commonly used fruit acids in anti-ageing products are lactic (from milk), malic (from apples), glycolic (from sugar cane) and pyruvic (from papaya). AHAs work by loosening the protein cement that glues the surface skin cells together, causing it to renew itself faster than it would naturally. Skin can look brighter and feels firmer. AHAs may also boost the natural production of the moisturising agent, hyaluronic acid, and promote collagen synthesis, although there have been no clinical trials to support this as yet. AHAs basically act as a rapid exfoliant, loosening dead skin cells from the skin's surface by dissolving the natural glue-like substance which binds these cells together. Once the old cells have been removed, fresh, new skin cells are exposed, giving the skin a smoother appearance. You can create a similar effect by gently rubbing your face with a damp flannel or muslin cloth.

Some manufacturers claim that AHAs can work wonders with acne and hyper-pigmentation. They are thought to be particularly useful for those with oily skin as the dissolving effect of the AHAs regulates the flow of the skin's natural oil. Older, dryer skins may also benefit from using AHAs as the removal of dry, flaky patches on the skin's surface, makes the skin more receptive to moisturisers. Many self-tanning lotions also contain fruit acids to loosen the dead skin cells on the surface which could block the staining action.

Cosmetic products contain between one and ten per cent AHA, with the lowest being the least effective. The disadvantage is that low levels of AHAs may have no effect, but high levels can be extremely irritating. Any AHA cream should be used with caution and discontinued should sensitivity occur. AHAs are acids after all, so it is not surprising that those with sensitive skin may experience a slight tingling or redness after applying creams that contain them. If your skin becomes seriously inflamed or irritated then you should stop using the product immediately. Many of the creams containing AHAs are expensive and it is worth while trying a test sample (if available) before splashing out on a whole bottle. Several of the recipes in this book include natural AHAs, including lactic acid from buttermilk and yoghurt, and glycolic acid from sugar and honey.

Allantoin

Derived from animal or plant sources, the main plant sources are comfrey root and wheatgerm. It is commonly used in skin-soothing cosmetics because of its ability to relieve inflammation and stimulate the growth of healthy skin. Allantoin also has moisturising properties.

Alum

This is a compound of ammoniun, sodium or potassium and is used as an astringent in skin tonics. Large concentrations of alum are toxic although it is thought that the levels commonly used in cosmetics are not harmful. For a gentler alternative, there are many astringent herbs such as witch hazel, calendula and chamomile.

Amino Acids

These are the building blocks of protein and are widely used in moisturisers to help water penetrate the skin.

Antioxidants (vitamins C, E and beta-carotene)

Antioxidants are said to work on the skin's surface in much the same way as they work internally, by neutralising harmful free radicals created by sunlight, pollution and cigarette smoke. Free radicals can cause severe damage both to our skin and within the body by attacking our cells on a molecular level. In fact, free radical damage has been linked to degenerative diseases such as heart disease, cancer and the ageing process itself. Every time we step outdoors our skin is subjected to increased levels of ageing free radicals from the sun's ultra-violet rays. This is why it is so important to wear a protective sunblock cream when exposed to the sun. Free radicals are also created within the skin as a result of pollutants (including car fumes and cigarette smoke) that settle on the skin's surface. They actively damage the skin in several different ways: by destroying the membranes surrounding skin cells, causing their contents to leak out and disintegrate, and encouraging the breakdown of collagen and elastin fibres that support the skin. Without this underlying support, our skin begins to slacken and sag.

Fortunately, the antioxidant nutrients can help protect our skin against free radical damage and increasingly more skincare creams contain these very special nutrients. Vitamin E is often used in moisturisers, sunscreens and anti-ageing creams because of its healing effect on skin and is probably one of the most useful antioxidants to look out for. However, choose creams containing natural, rather than synthetic or acetate vitamin E as this is at least a third more potent.

Vitamin C is another powerful antioxidant and it also stimulates the production of collagen which is essential for firm, supple skin. However, vitamin C is notoriously unstable and is difficult to use in skin creams, although some of the big brands claim to successfully include it. Many of my recipes for skin nourishing creams are naturally rich in important antioxidants, such as avocado oil which is high in both beta-carotene and vitamin E.

Beta Glucan

This is derived from yeast and said to repair sun-damaged skin by stimulating the body's immune system to produce healthy skin. It is claimed to regenerate collagen and elastin and reduce the appearance of wrinkles. These claims are not yet founded, although using brewer's yeast in home-made skin treatments may be useful.

Boric Acid

This acid comes from an alkaline salt called borax and it has antiseptic and anti-fungal properties. It is often used in eye creams and skin fresheners despite warnings about its toxicity from the American Medical Association.

Ceramides

Naturally present in the skin's own sebum, these are lipids (fats) that help to form a water-resistant seal over the stratum corneum — our outermost layer of skin. Creams containing ceramides claim to reinforce the skin's moisture barrier and improve its appearance and they are certainly good moisturisers.

Chitin

This is extracted from crab and mollusc shells. It retains water well and bonds with the skin's keratin to form a flexible, protective film. Not suitable for vegetarians.

Collagen

This is a substance which gives skin its structure and support and without it our skin would sag. It is implied that by adding collagen to anti-ageing creams, it will replenish our own skin's dwindling supply. In fact it is impossible for the collagen molecule to reach the dermis (the skin's deepest layer) except by injections, since it is much too large. The collagen used in skin creams is extracted from cow's hide, and it helps to hold water in the skin by forming a gel-like film on the surface, giving skin a smoother, firmer feeling. Not suitable for vegetarians.

D-panthenol

Otherwise known as pro-vitamin B5, D-panthenol is included in many skin and haircare products. It is necessary for the normal functioning of the skin and has a moisturising effect. D-panthenol also helps stimulate cellular renewal and new tissue growth.

Deoxyribonucleic Acid (DNA)

This is the basic component of all living matter and controls cell mechanisms. The DNA used in cosmetic products comes from plant, cow and sheep cells and, although it can't replace human DNA, it acts as an effective moisturiser. Not suitable for vegetarians.

Elastin

Like collagen, elastin is included in skin creams to help reinforce our own supplies. As its name suggests, elastin fibres give our skin its strength and elasticity. But again, elastin molecules cannot penetrate to the lowest layers of the skin. It is extracted from cow's fat and is a good moisturiser. Not suitable for vegetarians.

Essential Fatty Acids (EFAs)

Namely gamma-linolenic and linoleic acid, these are vital components of all cell membranes and necessary for the production of prostaglandins, which play a vital role in keeping skin healthy. Although best taken internally (as vegetable oils and evening primrose or borage oil supplements), when applied directly to the skin they help to stem water loss. These natural oils are a good base for moisturising lotions and creams.

Essential Oils

These are the fragrant, volatile and highly concentrated essences extracted from the leaves, flowers, roots and bark of plants. Each essential oil has moisturising properties and other important skin benefits. Jasmine, juniper berry, pine, spruce, rosemary and sandalwood oils have all been observed to stimulate fibroblast growth from 10-100 per cent. Fibroblast cells are present in connective tissue and are responsible for the production of the precursors of collagen and elastin which keep our skin firm and supple.

Glycerol

Derived from animal or vegetable fats, glycerol is included in many moisturisers to act as a shield against moisture loss. It also absorbs moisture from the air and forms a surface film on the skin without clogging the pores. If you would prefer to use products which do not contain animal ingredients, look out for the vegetable variety of glycerol on product labels.

Hyaluronic Acid

This is one of the Natural Moisturising Factors (NMFs) found naturally in the lowest levels of the dermis, where it forms part of the tissue that surrounds our collagen and elastin fibres. It is able to hold up to 200 times its own weight in water and makes an excellent moisturiser. Because of this it has a smoothing action on the skin and is a useful ingredient in many brands of skin cream.

Liposomes

These first appeared in the eighties and were heralded a major breakthrough, allowing active ingredients to penetrate deeper into the skin by 'carrying' them to their destiny, then slowly releasing them. Liposomes are tiny bubbles made up of a lipid (fatty) layer and a water layer, then filled with an active ingredient – such as vitamin E. There is some evidence that liposomes can give longer-lasting moisturising effects, due to their slow-release action, but there is controversy over whether they can penetrate the epidermis or upper levels of the skin. Nanospheres are simply a smaller version of liposomes, claimed to penetrate deeper into the skin thanks to their tiny size.

Phospholipids

Phospholipids such as lecithin, from soya beans or egg yolk are found in cell membranes and help to keep them healthy and watertight. As we age, these phospholipids become depleted, so by adding them to creams, manufacturers claim, the balance is restored. Whether this is true is not fully proven, but they do help to make good moisturisers, particularly for older skin. Recipes that use lecithin include my Remoisturising Mask on page 84.

Retinol

This is a derivative of vitamin A and is included in anti-ageing products under the pretext of helping repair damaged skin. It is thought to work by rebuilding damaged collagen and elastin and thereby improving the condition of the support structure of the skin - reducing wrinkles and lines. Retinol is not an antioxidant; only the vegetable form of vitamin A known as beta-carotene has this capacity. It is also not as powerful as its cousin Retin A. Scientific evidence suggests that Retin A can actually work on the skin's dermis (deepest layer) to rebuild damaged collagen and elastin – thereby reducing wrinkles and lines.

Sorbitol

Like glycerol, sorbitol is an humectant which means that it helps to preserve the moisture content of materials. It is found naturally in some berries and is used in moisturisers, deodorants, shampoos and hair sprays.

Superphycodismatuse (SPD)

This is a substance obtained from seaweed or algae that grow at a depth of 20 metres below the sea. It is thought to act powerfully against free radicals – thus protecting the skin cells which eventually form collagen and elastin against free radical damage. Seaweed has a similar mineral content to the sea itself which is almost identical to the water encased within each of our cell walls. The healthy functioning of each cell depends upon the healthy contents of its surrounding fluid and algae extracts are thought to have a purifying effect on skin cells and are included in many commercial cellulite treatments.

NEW GENERATION HEALERS

Some of the most exciting developments in skincare have stemmed from scientific research into naturally active ingredients.

Echinacea

This remarkable herb may be little known in Britain, but in Germany and America it is famous for its ability to boost the immune system as well as for its beneficial effects on the skin. Echinacea, pronounced eck-in-ace-ea, was first used by the North American Indians to treat a vast range of ailments from burns, wounds and snakebite to, flu and other viruses. Then in 1870 a Nebraskan doctor, H.C.F. Meyer, patented his own echinacea medicine and called it Meyer's Blood Purifier. By the 1930s echinacea was a popular herbal medicine in America and Europe. However, interest in the plant waned in favour of new antibiotics and has only been renewed in the last fifteen years. In America, echinacea reigns supreme as the most popular herb among medical herbalists and in Germany, there are over 200 echinacea products available, from tinctures to boost the immune system to creams to treat skin conditions such as acne and psoriasis.

Since the 1930's there have been over 200 studies into the properties of echinacea. These studies show that echinacea is not only a powerful immune-boosting herb when taken internally, but that it also has many beneficial effects on the skin when applied topically. Firstly, echinacea strengthens cell membranes against assault by invading microorganisms and therefore helps to prevent infection. This supports echinacea's initial use for the treatment of wounds. In addition, it stimulates new tissue growth and so further aids the wound healing process.

Echinacea also has an anti-inflammatory effect on the skin and has proved to be an effective treatment for inflammatory skin conditions such as eczema and psoriasis. It also possesses important anti-ageing properties. Echinacea stimulates the production of fibroblasts – the cells that eventually form collagen and elastin fibres – helping to keep our skin firm, smooth and wrinkle free. Echinacea is probably the most important of all skin-saving herbs.

Ginseng

This ancient herb has been used in Chinese medicine for centuries. There are many different varieties of ginseng – American, Chinese, Korean and Siberian – and it has recently gained great popularity in the West due to its health benefits. When taken internally, ginseng increases stamina and helps the body cope with physical stress which explains why athletes often take it. Studies have also shown that ginseng can improve our mental agility, particularly our ability to solve problems. Ginseng contains a group of chemicals called saponins which may account for its health benefits, as well as vitamins B1 and B2 and various minerals, including manganese, copper, and sulphur which all help to create firm, healthy skin. Ginseng in now used in some skincare preparations and has a stimulating, strengthening and protective effect on the skin. It is also thought that ginseng helps to soften the skin and increase its elasticity.

Gingko Biloba

This plant extract comes from a tree that originated in China over 200 million years ago. Gingko biloba trees are now grown throughout the world in temperate regions and live as long as a thousand years. The leaves of the tree contain a unique blend of active compounds, including flavonoids which have antioxidant and anti-inflammatory properties. Studies have shown that gingko biloba extract protects our capillary walls, combats the effects of destructive free radicals and increases blood circulation. It has been used therapeutically to treat cardiovascular problems, memory loss and cerebral insufficiency (poor blood supply to the brain) and is now cropping up in some skincare ranges.

Gingko biloba has a moisturising effect on the skin and also helps to stimulate

microcirculation. This enables the skin cells to absorb the nutrients they need from our blood while aiding the removal of waste from the cells. It is due to this stimulatory effect on our circulation that gingko is currently under investigation for use in cellulite smoothing creams. A sluggish circulation is thought to be a contributory factor in the formation of cellulite.

HINTS ON CHOOSING SKINCARE

Confronted with row after row of skincare brands, each subdivided into products for particular skin types, shopping for skincare products can be a confusing business. In Britain we spend some £400 million a year on facial skincare products, and by far the fastest growing area is anti-ageing creams and serums. It doesn't take a mathematician to calculate that we can save a great deal of money by making our own blends.

But while around seventy per cent of skincare products bought are moisturisers, relatively few of us buy or use cleansers. Despite advice from dermatologists, as many as sixty-five per cent of women are thought to use soap and water on their face from time to time. Soap is alkaline in nature, and upsets the skin's natural acidic balance, making it feel tight and dry, and it takes a while for the skin to redress the balance. Many conventional bar soaps are also heavily scented with synthetic fragrances and fixatives which may irritate the skin. If you're a soap and water addict, stick to the new soap-free cleansing bars or make a skin-friendly soap rich in natural ingredients from one my many recipes.

Although making your own natural beauty treatments is fun and guarantees that what you put on your skin contains high concentrations of naturally active ingredients, for convenience sake you will probably need to have some commercial products as a back-up.

One of the first criteria in choosing a product will be price. You can pay anything from £1 to £100 for a moisturiser, but is it worth spending a lot? With the more expensive brands you're paying for higher quality ingredients, the technology which created the new 'special' ingredients, the elegant packaging and image and usually a better texture. But in terms of what the product will actually do for your skin, the benefits of using a very expensive product are less clear. In recent years the technological advances used in premium brands have been filtering through to the cheaper brands with increasing speed. It's now true that you can get virtually the same benefits from a product costing £10 as one selling for £40. In a consumer study of anti-ageing creams in France, a budget vitamin E anti-wrinkle cream came out top for performance, despite being one of the cheapest brands tested.

The key is to have high levels of naturally active ingredients. Be guided by how the product feels on your skin and look out for good levels of antioxidant vitamins and some of the herbs mentioned above, on the labels.

Cleansers come in a confusing number of choices: creams, lotions, rinse-off gels and soap-free bars. You can also buy combined cleansers and toners, which can save you time and money if you like using toner. Soap and water will cleanse off water-soluble dirt, but its alkaline nature can upset the skin's natural pH balance, leaving it dry and tight. It is also not effective for dissolving all oil-based make-up or the skin's own sebum.

The first rule of a cleanser is that it should remove all impurities such as oil, grime, make-up and loose dead skin cells with ease. The second is that it shouldn't leave a residue, which can clog up pores and lead to spots. The rest is up to you. In general, wash-off cleansers are best suited to oilier skin types and cream-based to drier skins. If you have sensitive skin, avoid soap, fragrance and colour. One of the best universal cleansers is an oil-based formula, which removes make-up and dirt, and suits all skin types, even the sensitive. I have included many recipes for oil-based cleansers and I have found them to be both gentle and effective.

A moisturiser should be easily absorbed and not leave a greasy film on your skin. It's a good idea to go for one that gives a longer lasting effect, so you won't need to keep reapplying. Above all, choose one that includes a non-chemical sunscreen in it, unless you're happy to apply a separate sunscreen on top. Consultant dermatologist at St Thomas' Hospital Dr John Hawk recommends using one with no more than SPF10-15. 'If you use anything higher than that on a regular basis then you increase your risk of sensitivity,' he says. If you know you have sensitive skin, choose one which is fragrance and colour-free. Whether you choose cream, lotion, gel or oil is purely personal. In general, drier skins should opt for slightly thicker moisturisers, while oily skins should stick with more fluid products.

From 1997, all manufacturers should be legally bound to list all ingredients on the packs, which should help dissipate some of the hype about certain products and their 'exclusive' ingredients. This is particularly good news for those who are allergic to certain ingredients as it will be easier to avoid the allergens. Most reputable manufacturers will be introducing comprehensive ingredients listing well before this date. If you have sensitive skin look for products with as few chemicals and preservatives as possible. Even the most seemingly natural of skincare ranges are often packed with chemical sunscreens and petrochemicals to prolong shelf life.

Petrochemicals, such as mineral oils, are cheap, bland ingredients used in most commercial skincare. However, they do not contain any active ingredients, whereas plant oils are a rich source of nutrients. Alcohol, which is present in many products, can also cause problems for those with sensitive skins, so look out for alcohol-free products.

ANTI-AGEING EXTRAS
It should be remembered that fine facial lines are an inevitable – and natural – part of the ageing process.

Eye Creams
The eyes are usually the first area where lines appear and can cause concern. In the past few years eye creams have grown from nothing to an important money-spinner – every skincare range now seems to have one. Most claim to hide the appearance of fine lines, reduce puffiness and generally smooth the eye area to make the signs of ageing less noticeable. The basic ingredients of eye creams and moisturisers are the same, though eye creams usually contain more oil to help minimise fine lines. These creams may also go through more stringent ophthalmic testing to make sure they won't irritate the sensitive eye area. Eye creams are very quickly absorbed and won't leave a greasy film which could make eyes puffy. Key natural ingredients to look for include eyebright (a soothing herb), aloe vera and allantoin.

Firming Serums
These are designed to be used occasionally to give skin an instant boost. Basically they are 'super' moisturisers and by holding water on to the skin's surface they have a temporary firming, plumping and smoothing effect. However, because they are very rich (and expensive!), keep them for special occasions or when your skin is in need of a lift. Ingredients include proteins to give a tightening effect, vitamins E and A, moisturising agents such as essential oils, soothing plant extracts such as echinacea, and liposomes. Freshly made face packs are a useful alternative to give the complexion an instant boost.

Night Creams
Night creams are nothing new – 30 years ago women used to put cold cream on their faces before going to bed. The new ones tend to contain more active ingredients than daily moisturisers, since skin is supposedly more receptive and cell renewal is highest when we're resting. They also tend to be richer (or thicker) and this is more acceptable for night-time use. Night creams are not essential, but can be beneficial for drier skin types. If your skin is oily or combination, your normal daytime moisturiser will do just as well. However, one advantage of night creams is that they do not contain unnecessary sunscreens and usually have a higher concentration of useful herbal and vitamin extracts. My Rich Geranium Moisturiser is an excellent example of a good night cream and you can find this recipe on page 95.

CLEANSERS AND
SKIN TONICS

The starting point for a clear, glowing complexion is an efficient cleanser. One of the earliest recorded skin cleansers is cold cream. Originally invented by the Greek physician Galen, his recipe was based on beeswax, olive oil and rosewater. Cold cream gets its name because it is cooling on the skin and works as a cleanser when the oil and wax melt on to the face to loosen dirt, make-up and sebum. These can then be removed swiftly with tissues or a hot, damp facecloth to leave the skin feeling clean and soft. Modern versions of cold cream replace olive oil with cheaper mineral oil and the beeswax is replaced with a variety of synthetic substitutes. However, the original cold cream is easy to make at home and is an excellent cleanser for very dry skin that is easily upset and irritated by washing with soap and water.

Cold Cream Cleanser

2.5 ml (^{1}/$_2$ tsp) lecithin
    granules
    (or 3 lecithin capsules)
40 ml (8 tsp) rosewater
20 g (^{3}/$_4$ oz) beeswax
40 ml (8 tsp) olive oil
80 ml (3 fl oz) almond oil
4 drops rose essential oil
    (rosewood or rose
    geranium oils are less
    expensive and may be used
    instead)

This thick, rich cream has the sweet scent of honey and roses and is also a soothing skin moisturiser. In addition, it is useful as a baby's barrier cream, hand cream and rich, fragrant body cream.

● Dissolve the lecithin granules, or the contents of the capsules, in the rosewater. This may take several hours and could be left overnight.

● Put the beeswax, olive oil and almond oil in a heatproof bowl and place in a saucepan half filled with water. Bring the water to the boil, stirring the wax mixture continuously.

● When the wax has completely melted, stir the lecithin and rosewater solution into the mixture. Remove from the heat and stir well until the mixture cools.

● Beat to a smooth paste and add the drops of essential oil and mix again.

● While the mixture is still soft, use a knife or spatula to transfer the cream into small, airtight jars. Scrape the sides of the container to remove all traces of the cream before it solidifies.

Simple Cold Cream

90 ml (6 tbsp) almond oil
35 g (1^1/$_4$ oz) beeswax
250 ml (8 fl oz) very hot
    water
10 ml (2 tsp) borax
6 drops of your favourite
    essential oil

Because of its borax content it is wise to avoid using this cream on infants or on areas of broken skin.

● Melt the oil and wax together. Add the hot water and beat in the borax powder which acts as a natural emulsifier.

● Add a few drops of your chosen essential oil for a refreshing, natural fragrance.

NATURE'S CLEANSERS

Simple soap and water are amongst the oldest type of skin cleansers and are still the number-one method of cleaning the skin throughout the world. Soap is an alkaline substance made from animal or vegetable fats, mixed with caustic soda and sodium salts for bars of soap, and potassium salts in liquid soaps. Soap was first documented by the Ancient Egyptians, who made it from the soapwort plant, which is characterised by its unusual ability to foam in water. Native to Asia and parts of Europe, soapwort is an attractive plant with reddish, fragrant flowers and is still used as the basis of some of the more expensive vegetable soaps. Most modern soaps are more likely to contain beef tallow mixed with vegetable fats, such as coconut oil and palm kernel oil, which help them lather.

Milled soaps are the most common as they are the quickest and easiest to manufacture. They contain the highest proportion of animal fats, are highly alkaline and produce the most lather. The so-called superfatted soaps simply contain more oils or fats such as lanolin, olive oil or cocoa butter and are less likely to dry out the skin. However, all soaps tend to be strongly alkaline, with a pH value of between seven and ten. This can cause complexion problems because the surface of the skin is naturally acidic, with a pH value of 4.5 to 6.5. Washing with soap temporarily disrupts the delicate pH balance, disturbs the skin's natural oils and can lead to dryness and irritation.

Another problem with cleansing the face with soap is the washing water itself. Soap combines with the calcium and magnesium mineral deposits in hard water to leave an unattractive scum both around the rim of the basin and on your skin. This residue of soap suds can further dry and irritate the skin. Unless you live in a soft water area it is best to follow soap and water cleansing with a gentle skin tonic to remove any potentially irritating residues that remain.

Using soap to clean the face is really only a suitable option for those with combination or oily complexions. However, soap will not remove oil-based make-up, which is not soluble in water, so use a cream cleanser such as cold cream first. Medicated soaps can also cause problems when their antiseptic properties overly dry the skin. Side-effects of using medicated soaps on a regular basis include skin flaking, and mottling on the surface of coloured skins. They are also not particularly effective in combatting serious skin disorders such as acne. If you like using a medicated soap or have an oily, spotty complexion, try my recipe for Gently Medicated Soap (see page 76) that relies instead on gentler and time-tested antiseptic ingredients such as lavender and tea tree essential oils.

Other types of soap include transparent or glycerine soaps. These contain higher proportions of coconut oil or castor oil and are usually more moisturising. After manufacture, glycerine soaps need to be stored for several weeks to harden before being wrapped. Because they take longer to manufacture they invariably cost more. They are also not very good at producing a lather and are better suited to more sensitive skin, although they do end up sticking to the bottom of the soap dish.

Stylish soaps that can be made at home include exfoliating bars that contain tiny granules of sand, oatmeal or wheatgerm. These work by gently dislodging dead skin cells, leaving the skin thoroughly invigorating and glowing.

Oatmeal and Orange Soap Balls

275 g (10 oz) soft
   vegetable glycerine soap
   or Marseille block soap
50 g (2 oz) medium ground
   oatmeal
30 ml (2 tbsp) almond oil
5 ml (1 tsp) finely grated
   orange zest
12 drops lemon essential oil

The key to adapting soaps to
suit your own skin type is to
start with a good quality soap
as a base. Health shops and
herbal suppliers sell blocks of
vegetable glycerine soap. Most
other soaps are triple milled
which makes them difficult to
work with (they also contain
beef tallow, which smells terri-
ble when melted).

These old-fashioned soap balls
contain oatmeal, which is mildly exfoliating and moisturising
on the skin.

● Prepare the soap by slicing or
grating into small pieces.
● Melt in a double boiler or
heatproof bowl set over a pan
of simmering water. Stir in the
oatmeal and almond oil and
mix thoroughly.

● Remove from the heat, stir in
the grated orange zest and
lemon essential oil and allow
the mixture to cool slightly.
● Divide the mixture into four
equal-sized portions and roll
each one into a small ball.
● Place the soap balls on a wire
rack and leave overnight to
harden.
● When the soaps have set
hard, wrap in tissue paper and
store in a cool, dry place.

Gently Medicated Soap

150 g (5 oz) soft olive oil
   soap
50 ml (2 fl oz) strong sage
   tea
10 drops tea tree essential
   oil
10 drops lavender essential
   oil
5 ml (1 tsp) almond oil or
   jojoba oil (to grease
   moulds)

This is an excellent cleansing
bar to use on oily, combination
or acne-prone complexions.
The essential oils help purify
the skin and have a gentler
effect than many commercial
soaps. This recipe works best
with green olive oil soap from
Marseille, sold in health shops

● Chop or grate the soap into
small pieces. Place in a double-
boiler or heatproof bowl set
over a pan of simmering water
and begin to melt over a high
heat. Add the sage tea and stir
thoroughly, adding a little extra
water if necessary. Remove from
the heat and allow to cool
before adding the essential oils,
as heat reduces their potency.

● Pour the soap mixture into
greased moulds (such as small
bun tins, china ramekins or egg
cups) and leave in a cool place
to harden overnight.
● Remove from the moulds
using the tip of a sharp knife
and wrap in tissue paper until
ready to use. This soap remains
slightly soft even when stored

Richly Moisturising Soap

150 g (5 oz) good quality,
  unperfumed soap
15 ml (1 tbsp) coconut oil
50 ml (2 fl oz) strong
  chamomile tea
10 ml (2 tsp) olive oil
5 ml (1 tsp) honey
5 drops sandalwood or
  geranium essential oil
5 ml (1 tsp) almond or olive
  oil (to grease moulds)

Unlike many commercial soaps, this bar cleanses the skin thoroughly yet gently and leaves the skin feeling soft. It is gentle enough to use on babies' and children's sensitive skins.

● Chop or grate the soap into small pieces. Put in a double boiler or heatproof bowl set over a pan of simmering water, and melt with the coconut oil.
● Add the chamomile tea, olive oil and honey. Mix thoroughly and allow to cool. Add the sandalwood or geranium essential oil to fragrance the soap (or substitute your own favourite essence).
● Pour the mixture into greased moulds (as for Gently Medicated Soap, see page 76) and leave overnight in a cool place to harden.

Simple Soapwort Cleanser

10 g (¼ oz) finely chopped
  soapwort root
600 ml (1 pint) water
45 ml (3 tbsp) rosewater
  (optional)

Although it looks like cold tea, this is the simplest cleanser to make and works well on sensitive skins. It is great to use in the bath as it helps soften the water. It is also useful if you live in a hard water area, as regular soaps often react with the alkaline mineral deposits in the water and leave a scum on the skin. Soapwort root is available from good herbal suppliers.

● Place the chopped soapwort root in a small saucepan and pour on the water. Bring to the boil, turn the heat down, cover and simmer on a low heat for 15-20 minutes.
● This mixture gives off a strange smell while simmering, which can be disguised by adding the optional rosewater (use triple-distilled rosewater for a stronger scent).
● Remove the pan from the heat and allow to cool.

● Strain the mixture through a coffee filter or muslin cloth to remove the soapwort pieces and bottle the remaining liquid.
● To use, shake well and pour a small amount into the palm of the hand, then massage into the skin before rinsing with plenty of warm water.

Chamomile Cleanser

40 g (1½ oz) cocoa butter
75 ml (3 fl oz) almond oil
10 drops chamomile
   essential oil

This rich cleanser is an excellent make-up remover. It is suitable for all skin types, including dry and sensitive. It is also good for oily complexions as the oils in the cream dissolve the skin's own sebum and remove grease from the surface of the skin. Try using it as a weekly treatment for problem areas such as blackheads around the nose and chin.

● First, melt the cocoa butter in a small saucepan over a low heat. Alternatively, melt in the microwave by zapping on 'High' for three minutes or so. Remove from the heat and stir in the almond oil. Whisk in the chamomile essential oil. Pour into a clean, airtight jar.

● To use, rub a small amount of the cleansing cream into the face and neck, massaging in gentle circular movements with the fingertips. Remove with a clean cotton cloth, such as a baby's muslin, or soft face flannel wrung out in hot water. Rinse the cloth and repeat until all traces of the cleanser have been removed. Dip the cloth into cold water and pat over the face and neck to tighten the skin. Used regularly, this chamomile cleanser will help to soften and remove blackheads and will help to keep the skin sparklingly clear.

Kaolin Cleanser

5 ml (1 tsp) Fuller's earth
15 ml (1 tbsp) warm water
5 ml (1 tsp) finely ground
   oatmeal
2 drops lavender or
   geranium essential oil

This is a favourite cleanser of mine for oily, combination and acne-prone skins which smells good and works well. However, it does not keep, so cover with a small amount of water to prevent it from drying out, unless you plan to use it immediately.

● Combine the Fuller's earth with the warm water and mix to a smooth paste. Stir in the oatmeal and lavender or geranium essential oil.
● To use, pin hair back from the face and apply to the skin using the fingertips, or a clean facial sponge.

● Allow to dry on the skin for one minute before rinsing off, using gentle massaging movements and plenty of warm rinsing water.
● Finally, remove any residues of cleanser with Floral Skin Freshener for oily skins (see page 79).

Honey Purifier

5 ml (2 tsp) honey
250 ml (8 fl oz) hot water

Sometimes the simplest beauty treatments are the best. This one is inexpensive and works well. Honey is naturally antiseptic and moisturising. Varieties of manuka honey are made with nectar from the tea tree and so are especially soothing to the skin.

This treatment is effective for all skin types and can be carried out once a week to help keep the complexion clear.
● Start by rubbing the honey into the face using small circular movements (runny honey is the easiest to use).

● Dip the fingertips into the hot water and repeat. The heat from the water will encourage the skin to soften and help shift embedded dirt and debris. After a few minutes of massage, rinse the face in clean, tepid water and pat dry.

Floral Skin Fresheners

200 ml (7 fl oz) carbonated
   mineral water
3 drops cider vinegar
normal skins: 3 drops lavender
   + 3 drops geranium
   essential oils
dry skins: 3 drops sandalwood
   + 3 drops chamomile
   essential oils
oily skins: 3 drops lemon + 3
   drops lavender essential
   oils

These floral waters are wonderfully refreshing on the face and are simple to tailor to your skin type. Unlike synthetic skin tonics they do not contain potentially irritating colourants, alcohol or preservatives.

● First, measure the mineral water and cider vinegar into a screw-top bottle or jar and add the appropriate essential oils drop by drop.

● Replace the top of the container and shake well to mix the oils. Apply with cotton wool to remove traces of cleanser from the face.

Invigorating Skin Tonic

120 ml (4 fl oz) witch hazel
50 ml (2 fl oz) rosewater
2 drops rose essential oil
(or rose geranium or
rosewood)

Witch hazel has a seemingly
pore-shrinking ability, due to
the natural tannins found in the
Hamamelis plant. These tannins
are also found in nettles and
nettle tea may be used instead
of witch hazel if this is easier.
Both varieties are excellent for
toning normal, combination
and oily skins.

● Place the ingredients in a
screw-top bottle or jar and
shake well.
● Use as a skin tonic to remove
all traces of cleanser and soap-
sud residues from the face and
neck.

Alum Astringent

5 ml (1 tsp) alum crystals
250 ml (8 fl oz) warm
water
120 ml (4 fl oz) witch hazel

A true astringent contracts skin
tissues, so if you dab a bit on
the end of your tongue it will
not only taste bitter but you
should also feel the skin pucker.
This astringent skin tonic is
highly effective and can be
made for a fraction of the price
of shop-bought lotions. It's
especially good for spot-prone
teenage skins.
Alum is a form of aluminium
crystals and can be found in
chemists.

● Dissolve the alum in the
water, add the witch hazel and
mix well. Store in a screw-top
bottle or jar, away from heat
and light.

Refreshing Spritzer

120 ml (4 fl oz) carbonated
mineral water
2 drops peppermint
essential oil
3 drops neroli essential oil

This instant skin refresher is
especially useful during hot
weather and can also be sprayed
over foundation and powder to
set it in place.

● Place all the ingredients in a
screw-top bottle or jar and
shake well. Transfer the liquid
to a plastic spray bottle with a
fine mist pump (available from
most chemists and department
stores).

● Store in the fridge and use to
lightly spritz over the face and
neck. Avoid spraying the eyes.

Extremely Gentle Skin Freshener

10 ml (2 tsp) dried
   chamomile flowers or
   1 tea bag
120 ml (4 fl oz) rosewater
50 ml (2 fl oz) aloe vera
   juice
2 drops sandalwood essential
   oil

Beware of commercial skin toners if your skin is dry or sensitive as they can contain high levels of alcohol used to evaporate the liquid from the skin. Even alcohol-free varieties contain other chemicals to achieve the same effect, and rob the skin of valuable moisture. Aloe vera juice is a fabulous ingredient for refreshing all skin types.

● Make the chamomile tea by infusing the dried chamomile flowers or tea bag in a cup of almost boiling water. Allow to cool and strain.

● Pour 120 ml (4 fl oz) of the tea into a screw-top bottle or jar and add the rosewater, aloe vera juice and sandalwood essential oil. Shake well to mix.
● Keep tightly sealed in a cool place – preferably in the fridge – and use within one week.

Barley Skin Freshener

75 g (3 oz) pot barley
750 ml (1¼ pints) water
4 drops lemon, bergamot or
   mandarin essential oil

This skin freshener is suitable for normal and combination complexions. It is based on barley water, which is a rich source of several trace minerals needed by the skin, including potassium, zinc and sulphur.

● Place the pot barley and the water in a saucepan and bring to the boil. Cover and simmer on a low heat for 30 minutes, or until the barley has completely cooked through.

● Strain the liquid and transfer to a screw-top bottle or jar (keep the pearl barley and use to enrich soups or stews).
● Add the citrus essential oil and shake well.
● Keep in the fridge and use after cleansing the face to refresh the skin.

PROBLEM SOLVERS AND SKIN SAVERS

All skin types will benefit from a special treatment once in a while. Face masks and skin scrubs are the fastest way to get the complexion glowing and they are quick and easy to make. The following recipes are split into sections according to skin type and at the end of this chapter you will also find advice and simple treatments for more serious skin disorders, such as acne.

Herbal Steams

15 ml (I tbsp) fresh or dried herb mixture:
normal skins: **lavender and sage**
dry skins: **chamomile and basil**
oily/combination skins: **mint and lemon peel**
bowl of hot water
large towel

A weekly herbal steam is a useful skin treatment for all skin types. It is suitable for dry and sensitive complexions as the moisture from the steam helps plump up dehydrated skin cells. It is also a good treatment for oily and combination skins, as the heat from the steam gently softens blackheads or hardened plugs of sebum that can clog the pores and cause spots.

● Simply fill a large bowl with water which has been boiled and cooled slightly. Stir in the herbs and allow to infuse for a few minutes (you can use herbal tea bags if fresh or dried herbs are not available).

● Place a large towel around your head and neck so that it forms a tent and lean over the bowl. Close the eyes and allow the steam to work on the skin for I-3 minutes.

● Do not have the water so hot that the steam scalds the skin — a gentle heat is all that is required.

● Afterwards, pat the skin dry with a cool, clean face cloth and apply a light moisturiser.

Re-Moisturising Mask

15 ml (I tbsp) buttermilk or plain, live yogurt
I egg yolk
2.5 ml ($^{1}/_{2}$ tsp) honey
5 ml (I tsp) mayonnaise

This rich, fluid moisturising mask contains natural lecithin from the egg yolk, which helps lock moisture into the skin. In addition, the buttermilk or yogurt contains lactic acid which is a natural AHA (alpha hydroxy acid). This means it gently loosens the cellular cement between surface skin cells and can help the skin appear fresher. Lactic acid also has good moisturising properties for the face, neck and hands and with regular use can help fade brown 'age' spots. Rachel's Dairy make an excellent organic buttermilk which can be found in good health shops.

● Mix all the ingredients in a bowl to form a smooth paste. Apply to clean, dry skin on the face and neck and leave for 15-20 minutes.

● Rinse thoroughly with plenty of warm water and pat dry.

● A simpler version of this emollient mask may be made by mixing 2.5 ml ($^{1}/_{2}$ tsp) honey with one egg yolk. The honey forms a moisturising film on the face while the lecithin in the egg yolk is also deeply nourishing and helps bind moisture on to the skin.

Oatmeal and Mint Refresher

60 ml (4 tbsp) finely ground
  oatmeal
50 ml (2 fl oz) hot water
15 ml (1 tbsp) fresh mint
  leaves

This refreshingly fragrant face
mask contains fresh peppermint
to pep up the skin and oatmeal
to gently soothe minor irritations. This amount will make
enough for two masks, or the
remainder can be used on the
body before a shower.

● Mix the oatmeal with the
hot water until it forms a rich,
thick paste.

● Wash and finely chop the
mint leaves and add to the oatmeal. Leave for a few minutes
for the oatmeal to absorb the
water and mint extracts before
applying to freshly cleansed
skin on the face and neck.
● Relax for 20 minutes before
rinsing away with warm water
and damp cotton wool or
muslin cloth. Gently pat the
skin dry and apply a light
moisturiser.

Queen Victoria's Face Pack

50 g (2 oz) barley flour or
  brown rice flour
15 ml (1 tbsp) runny honey
1 egg white, lightly beaten

This recipe is similar to one
used by the Royal Court during
Queen Victoria's reign. It has a
firm texure with an attractive
soft scent and is excellent for
refining and moisturising the
complexion while tightening
slack skin tissues.

● In a small bowl, gradually mix
the flour with the runny honey
and the egg white until the mixture forms a stiff paste.

● Smooth on to clean skin over
the face and neck. Relax for
15-20 minutes before rinsing
with cool water.
● Gently pat the skin dry and
apply a light moisturiser.

Banana Skin Pack

I small ripe banana
   (preferably organic or
   un-gassed)
25 g (I oz) finely ground
   oatmeal
5 ml (I tsp) runny honey

This gentle, fruity face mask is easy to make and is excellent for re-moisturising and soothing tired, dehydrated skins. It also brings a bloom to tired, sallow or grey complexions. I prefer to use organically grown or un-gassed bananas (the gas is used to artificially ripen most bananas) as these do not have traces of chemicals on their skins which could end up on my skin.

● Mash the banana thoroughly in a small bowl until it forms a smooth paste.

● Stir in the finely ground oatmeal and runny honey. Mix together well before applying to freshly cleansed skin on the face and neck.
● Relax for 15-20 minutes before rinsing off using warm water.
● Pat the skin dry with a soft towel and apply a light moisturising cream.

Combination Skin Mask

15 ml (I tbsp) finely
   ground oatmeal
15 ml (I tbsp) live, plain
   yogurt
1/2 apple, freshly grated
10 ml (2 tsp) fresh lemon
   juice

A good facial mask, full of the tangy natural AHA's which are found in many popular commercial skin creams. This recipe is best suited to combination skins as the enzymatic action of the fresh apple and lemon juice helps tighten pores and also acts as a gentle exfoliant, dislodging dead skin cells and removing sebum build-up. The mask is especially useful for slightly irritated or blotchy skins, as the oatmeal has a soothing effect. Make sure the yogurt contains acidophilus, as this type of beneficial bacterium is the most useful when it comes to clearing up spots and pimples.

● Mix the oatmeal with the yogurt to form a paste. Add the grated apple and lemon juice and stir well.
● Apply to clean, dry skin on the face and neck. Relax for 15-20 minutes before rinsing thoroughly with warm water and patting the skin dry.

SCRUBBING UP

Our skin is constantly changing as fresh, young cells are formed to replace dead cells on the skin's surface. As the older skin cells die off they can easily clog the pores and lead to a dull, sallow-looking complexion. Exfoliation is the term given to any type of treatment that gently removes the top layer of dead skin cells, such as a skin scrub. Other kinds of effective exfoliators include soaps with gritty granules, facial brushes, abrasive creams, flannels, loofahs and even clay-based face masks that dislodge dead cells and remove them from the skin. An exfoliating treatment should always be extremely gentle — if you are too zealous you may end up with a face full of broken veins.

Young skins can use a scrub twice a week to keep the complexion clear of blemishes, while more mature skins should stick to a once-weekly treatment. However, older skins do benefit from exfoliation, as it also helps speed up the rate at which fresh, young skin cells are replaced and this leads to a younger-looking complexion. Always avoid the fragile eye area, though, and be sure to apply a moisturiser after each treatment.

Dingy Skin Scrub

15 ml (1 tbsp) medium ground oatmeal
30 ml (2 tbsp) rose water
5 ml (1 tsp) granulated sugar
5 ml (1 tsp) honey

This appetising mixture is my favourite weekly treatment and will brighten and refine all skin types. The oatmeal helps soothe the skin while the sugar buffs away dead skin cells and also has a mildly anti-bacterial effect.

● Mix all the ingredients together in a bowl until they form a gritty paste. Apply to clean skin using gentle circular movements with the fingertips.
● Concentrate on the nostrils, chin and forehead to dislodge dead skin cells and unclog the pores. Take care not to rub too hard - the smallest amount of pressure is all that is needed to dislodge flakes of dry, dingy-looking skin.

Fruity Exfoliator

1 ripe papaya

This works by the enzymatic action of papain found in papaya fruit which dissolves dead keratin, the hardened protein found in dead skin cells. The treatment relies on papain to literally eat up dead, dingy skin that makes the skin look sallow and can lead to spots.

● Slice the papaya in half and peel away the skin in large pieces.

● Rub the inside of the skin over a freshly cleansed face and neck, massaging over the forehead, nose and chin for 1-2 minutes. Rinse the skin with clean, cool water and pat dry.
● This treatment is good to use before a moisturising face mask as it lifts off the dead surface cells so the face mask can penetrate the skin more easily.

Sensitive Skin Lotion

250 ml (8 fl oz) water
25 g (1 oz) dried
  marshmallow root

Marshmallow is an excellent skin-soothing herb and has been traditionally used by herbalists for centuries to help heal minor skin blemishes and irritations. Dried pieces of the root are available from all good herbal suppliers.

● Boil the water and pour over the marshmallow pieces. Leave overnight to soak.

● Discard the pieces of root and pass the liquid through a fine muslin cloth or paper coffee filter. You should end up with approximately 90 ml (6 tbsp) of rich, dark marshmallow extract.

● Transfer the strained liquid to a clean screw-top bottle or jar. Apply daily to the affected area using cotton wool. Store the lotion in a cool, dark place such as the fridge.

Red-Face Compress

15 ml (1 tbsp) finely ground
  oatmeal
60 ml (4 tbsp) warm water
2 drops chamomile essential
  oil
piece of muslin cloth or
  flannel

This treatment is especially good for faces that redden easily or become blotchy and irritated in cold weather. Oatmeal is especially soothing and some herbalists say it can help shrink blood vessels and so prevent tiny thread veins from forming.

● Finally, place the compress over the face, lie down and relax for 15 minutes. Remove the compress, rinse out in clear, cool water and dab over the skin to remove any oatmeal residue. Finally, pat the face and neck dry.

● Mix together the oatmeal and water and leave for a couple of minutes to thicken. Add the chamomile essential oil and stir well to combine.

● Dip the muslin cloth or flannel into the oatmeal mixture and gently pat over the skin. Repeat several times.

Puffy Eye Remedy

**2 strong tea bags
(e.g. Darjeeling)**

This treatment is simplicity itself and yet it can be more effective than some of the expensive eye gels. The natural tannins in the tea leaves tighten the skin tissues around the eye area and dramatically reduce signs of puffiness and swelling. The coldness of the refrigerated compress also stimulates the lymphatic system around the eye area and helps reduce puffiness too.

● Simply rinse the tea bags under the tap and refrigerate for 30 minutes. Apply to clean eyelids and relax for 20 minutes before removing.

Scar Tissue Lotion

**15 ml (1 tbsp) rose hip oil
15 ml (1 tbsp) wheatgerm
oil
3 drops sandalwood
essential oil**

Rose hip oil is a fabulous skin healer. It is available from good health shops or from aromatherapy suppliers and is sometimes sold under its Latin name of *Rosa rubiginosa.*
● Measure the oils into a small bottle or jar and shake to mix.
● Rub on to the affected area twice daily. This lotion has a naturally high vitamin E content and is also a good treatment to help fade stretchmarks, or for use on surgical wounds once the stitches have been removed.

Herbal Antiseptic Lotion

**10 g (¼ oz) marigold petals
10 g (¼ oz) dried golden
seal
10 g (¼ oz) dried pulsatilla
350 ml (12 fl oz) water**

This herbal antiseptic lotion is good for bruises and sprains and will keep in the fridge for several days.

● Mix the dried herbs and flower petals together. Place in a small saucepan together with the water and simmer for 15 minutes. Leave to cool.

● Strain the lotion and apply the liquid to the affected area avoiding broken skin.

Peppermint Skin Solution

**5ml (1 tsp) hazelnut or
jojoba oil
1 drop peppermint essential
oil**

A useful treatment for spotty and acne-prone skins. Peppermint essential oil from *Mentha piperata* is the best variety to use as it contains a high proportion of natural plant hormones which can help this skin condition.

● Mix the oils and dab on to the affected area twice daily.

Hazelnut or jojoba oils are the best carrier oils to use as they have excellent powers of penetration and are also slightly astringent, so suiting the oilier skin types.

Tea Tree Spot-Buster

**5 ml (1 tsp) hazelnut or
jojoba oil
2 drops tea tree essential oil
piece of muslin cloth or face
flannel**

An excellent treatment for stubborn spots on the face, neck and back. Before starting this treatment, it is essential to scrub the hands and nails thoroughly in soapy water so they are very clean.

● Firstly rinse the muslin cloth or face flannel in clean hot water, wring out and apply to the area that needs treating.
● When the cloth begins to cool, dip into hot water again, wring and repeat. The heat from the cloth gently softens spots, pimples and blackheads, dissolving the trapped sebum and releasing embedded grime.

● Next, mix together the oils in the palm of one hand and apply to the affected area with warm fingertips. Massage gently to bring fresh blood supplies to the surface of the skin, which will help carry trapped toxins away from beneath the skin. Leave overnight.

Herbal Oils

**15 ml (1 tbsp) flower petals
30 ml (2 tbsp) high quality
almond or olive oil**

Many useful skin oils such as calendula oil (from pot marigold petals) and St John's wort oil may be made by macerating the flowers in a pure vegetable oil.

● Collect together the flower petals, or dried petals from a herbal supplier, and sprinkle into the oil. Stir well, seal tightly and leave in a cool, dark place for 2-3 weeks.

● After this time the healing extracts from the oil sacs on the petals will have been absorbed into the oil and the mixture can be strained and re-bottled ready for use in massage blends on areas of problem skin.

INSTANT BEAUTY BOOSTERS

These ideas are for fast, natural face-fixers when time is tight.

Rapid Cleansers
● Use plain, live yogurt to cleanse the skin and remove dirt and make-up. Simply rub into the skin and splash off with tepid water.
● Mix together 15 ml (1 tbsp) finely ground oatmeal with 30 ml (2 tbsp) hot water, gently rub into the skin and rinse off.
● Use jojoba oil or grapeseed oil to shift stubborn waterproof mascara. Apply with a lightly dampened cotton wool pad.

Simple Skin Tonics
● Warm chamomile tea is an excellent toner for dry, sensitive skins.
● Pure rosewater makes a refreshing skin tonic. Try using it straight from the fridge.
● To remove soap-sud residues and restore the skin's natural pH (acid/alkaline) balance, mix 5 ml (1 tsp) cider vinegar into a large tumbler of cool water and splash over the face after cleansing.

Spot Busters
● Dab on neat acetone to dry up stubborn spots using a fresh cotton-tipped applicator for each pimple.
● Apply dots of milk of magnesia liquid to heal skin blemishes and acne lesions.
● Use neat witch hazel on a cotton wool ball to clear a spotty forehead or chin.

Open-Pore Tonics
● Apply a small quantity of neat vodka to the nose and chin area to tighten enlarged pores.
● A slice of lemon rubbed over the affected area helps open pores appear smaller and also fades freckles.

Skin Scruffers
● 15 ml (1 tbsp) granulated white sugar mixed with a few drops of hot water makes an excellent skin scrub for slightly spotty skins, as sugar contains mildly antibacterial properties.
● Before stepping into the shower, smooth olive oil over the body and rub in handfuls of finely ground sea salt for an invigorating all-over skin scrub.
● Massage a handful of coarsely ground oatmeal on the chest and upper arms while in the bath to leave the skin soft and glowing.

Speedy Skin Nourishers
● To re-moisturise a dry, sallow complexion, massage a generous dollop of fresh mayonnaise into the skin, leave for 10 minutes and rinse with cool water.
● A thin layer of sunflower or soya margarine serves as a good make-shift moisturiser.
● A small amount of almond oil or avocado oil will nourish the face and neck. Apply before bedtime and leave overnight to sink into the skin.

Moisturisers
and Skin Creams

Our skin makes its own moisturiser by mixing water with a natural oil called sebum, which is secreted by the sebaceous glands. Sebum is produced from these tiny glands that lie just beneath the surface of the skin, and flows along ducts into the hair follicles and on to the skin. Sebum itself is slightly acidic and has an anti-bacterial action to protect the skin from germs. The production of sebum is heavily influenced by our hormones, which is why skin types vary so much from person to person. Modern living also affects sebum and the overall moisture levels in our skin.

MOISTURE ROBBERS

Centrally heated environments and air-conditioned offices rob the complexion of the moisture it needs to stay supple and young looking. Extreme weather conditions such as the wind, sun and low humidity levels also conspire against the complexion and encourage dehydration. In addition, the skin's ability to retain moisture reduces with age, which is why our skin tends to become dryer as we get older. Other factors that deplete our natural moisture levels within the skin include smoking, alcohol and a diet low in essential fatty acids such as vegetable oils.

Using a moisturising cream is a good way of topping up the skin's moisture content, not by adding more oil, but by forming a protective film over the surface of the skin that prevents valuable water from escaping.

There are two main types of moisturising creams for the face and body. Water-in-oil emulsions are the richest form of cream that suit dry, sensitive and more mature skin types. These are especially useful during the winter months when the skin is more prone to flaking and chapping. The other type of cream is made with an oil-in-water formulation which means that it is lighter, more easily absorbed and suits normal, combination and oily skins (even oily complexions may need a light-weight moisturiser occasionally, as skin dehydration is caused by water evaporating from within the skin, not a lack of sebum on its surface). This type of lighter skin cream is more useful in the humid summer months as they generally contain humectants such as glycerine, which attracts moisture from the atmosphere. They are not so good in dry air conditions as they tend to attract precious moisture from the skin itself.

MODERN MOISTURISERS

These days, moisturisers have many added skin benefits. They may contain sunscreens that give the face anti-ageing protection from the sun's rays, an increasingly important consideration as the ozone layer thins above us. Skin creams may also contain soothing ingredients such as antiseptic herbal extracts to help heal irritations. They also help to shield the skin from atmospheric pollutants such as car fumes and cigarette smoke and comprise a very valuable barrier cream.

The best time to use a moisturiser is immediately after cleansing the face. If your skin is very dry you can apply a thin layer of cream to the skin while it is still damp as this helps trap extra moisture.

Night creams too, are useful if your skin is dry or showing visible signs of ageing. The best type of night creams are made with just a few simple ingredients, such as rejuvenating and soothing herbal extracts which have plenty of time to penetrate the skin overnight while we sleep.

Honey Bee Moisturiser

60 ml (4 tbsp) almond oil
60 ml (4 tbsp) avocado oil
50 g (2 oz) cocoa butter
5 ml (1 tsp) beeswax pieces
10 ml (2 tsp) runny honey
10 drops chamomile
  essential oil

This darkly nourishing cream smells delicious and is mildly anti-bacterial due to its honey content. This is a concentrated moisturiser so use sparingly. If you find that the honey starts to separate out simply stir it back into the mixture.

● Put the almond oil, avocado oil, cocoa butter and beeswax pieces in a heatproof bowl and place in a saucepan half-filled with water. Heat gently over a low flame until the cocoa butter and beeswax have melted.

● Remove from the heat and stir in the honey. Beat continuously with a metal spoon or palette knife while the mixture cools. Add the chamomile essential oil and pour into a small screw-top jar. Store in a cool, dark place.

Rich Geranium Moisturiser

60 ml (4 tbsp) avocado
  oil
60 ml (4 tbsp) wheatgerm
  oil
25 ml (1 fl oz) liquid lanolin
5 ml (1 tsp) beeswax pieces
2.5 ml (½ tsp) borax
  powder
30 ml (2 tbsp) rosewater
10-15 drops geranium
  essential oil

This has a rich colour and is a good, nourishing night treatment or it can be used as a daily moisturiser, suitable for even sensitive skins. It also makes a rich body lotion. For a lighter coloured cream, use almond oil instead of the darkly nourishing avocado oil.

● Put the avocado and wheatgerm oils together in a heat-proof bowl and place in a saucepan half-filled with water.

● Add the lanolin and beeswax pieces and heat gently until the mixture has completely melted.
● Meanwhile, dissolve the borax powder in the rosewater and add to the waxy mixture. Stir thoroughly, remove from the heat and add the geranium essential oil. Continue to stir the mixture until it is cool enough to pour into small screw-top jars.

Scented Cold Cream

90 ml (6 tbsp) almond oil
35 g (1¼ oz) beeswax
150 ml (5 fl oz) just-boiled
    water
10 ml (2 tsp) borax
10 drops of essential oil for
    fragrance

Cold cream has been faithfully used by women for hundreds of years to moisturise their skin at night. Here is my version of this time-honoured recipe. Because of its borax content, the cream should not be used on infants or broken skin.

● Melt the oil and wax in a pan on a medium heat. Add the hot water and borax and beat well. Then allow to cool.

● You can add perfume to the cream by mixing in a few drops of your favourite essential oil (sandalwood is my favourite and is especially good for dry and mature skins).

● Store the cream in a sealed container.

Chamomile Neck Cream

10 g (½ oz) beeswax pieces
50 g (2 oz) cocoa butter
45 ml (3 tbsp) almond or
    avocado oil
2 drops chamomile essential
    oil

This rich throat cream is especially suitable for using on areas of severely dehydrated skin such as the upper arms and elbows.

● Put the beeswax, cocoa butter and almond or avocado oil in a small saucepan. Melt over a high heat for 3½ minutes. Alternatively, melt in the microwave on 'High' for 4 minutes. Remove from the heat and add the chamomile essential oil.

● Continue to stir until the mixture is cool enough to be transferred to small screw-top jars. Seal each one with a disc of greaseproof paper.

● To use, scoop out a small amount and warm between the palms of the hands before smoothing on to the skin.

Sunscreen Oil

120 ml (4 fl oz) sesame oil
50 ml (2 fl oz) grapeseed oil
50 ml (2 fl oz) strong tea
    (e.g. Darjeeling)

This is a good sunscreening oil with a wonderfully nutty aroma. It is suitable for darker skins that tan easily, and can be used all over the body. However, the sun-filtering properties are not sufficient for those with fair skin, for children or for tropical climates.

Sesame oil has natural sunscreening properties and will shield the skin from about one-third of the sun's harmful rays. The tannins present in the tea also help block ultra-violet light.

● Pour the oils into a large, screw-top bottle, add the cooled tea and shake well.

● Shake the mixture vigorously before applying over face and body. Re-apply after swimming.

Oil-Free Moisturiser

20 g (¾ oz) linseeds
200 ml (7 fl oz) boiling
   water
15 ml (1 tbsp) glycerine
15 ml (1 tbsp) rosewater
1 drop neroli essential oil
   (optional)

Linseeds are an excellent source
of natural mucilage, a gel-like
paste that soothes the skin.

● Crack the linseeds open by
whizzing in a blender or coffee
grinder for a few seconds.
Transfer them to a small cup
and pour on the boiling water.
Stir continually while the linseeds steep as the mixture cools
down. Strain off the linseeds
and discard.

● Mix the linseed mucilage with
the glycerine and rosewater to
form a lightly moisturising
lotion. Add the neroli essential
oil to give the lotion the wonderful aroma of orange blossom.
● Apply to combination or oily
skins after cleansing.

Sensitive Skin Splash

120 ml (4 fl oz) rosewater
60 ml (4 tbsp) glycerine

This simple moisturising lotion
is an excellent soother for sensitive skins. It also makes a wonderful after-bath body splash
that leaves the skin smelling
sweet and feeling smooth.

Rosewater is available from
most chemists or can be made
by blending 25 ml (1 fl oz)
essence of roses with 4.5 litres
(8 pints) distilled water. Triple
distilled rosewater can also be
bought from a chemist and is
more concentrated.

● Whisk together the rosewater
with the glycerine. Store in a
tightly sealed bottle away from
heat and light. Shake gently
before use.

Cucumber Shaving Cream

175 g (6 oz) coconut oil
50 ml (2 fl oz) witch hazel
90 ml (6 tbsp) almond oil
1/2 cucumber, peeled
4 drops sandalwood essential
  oil
4 drops lavender essential oil

This subtly fragrant shaving cream is excellent for a man's bristly beard, or for softer hairs on feminine legs and underarms. It contains cucumber juice to soothe the skin, lavender oil to heal any razor nicks and natural plant oils to leave the skin moisturised and smooth.

● Melt the coconut oil slowly in a small saucepan over a low heat (coconut oil is solid at room temperature). Remove from the heat and stir in the witch hazel and almond oil.
● Whizz the cucumber in a blender and pass the liquid through a fine sieve. Add 15 ml (1 tbsp) of the juice to the mixture together with the sandalwood and lavender essential

oils. Mix thoroughly and pour into a screw-top jar.
● To use, stir the cream with the fingertips and apply to the skin. After shaving, remove any remaining traces of cream with a hot damp flannel and pat the skin dry. There is no need to follow with an additional moisturiser as the skin will be left feeling smooth and soft.

Note: this formula contains fresh cucumber extracts which means it should be kept in a cool place and has a limited shelf-life. Stir before each use.

Moisturising Eye Balm

10 ml (2 tsp) avocado oil
10 ml (2 tsp) wheatgerm oil
10 ml (2 tsp) calendula oil
2.5 ml (1/2 tsp) runny honey
10 g (1/4 oz) cocoa butter

This mixture uses pure plant oils and honey to boost the moisture content of the fragile skin tissues surrounding the eye area. The honey is important because it is rich in

natural sugars that are similar to the skin's own Natural Moisturising Factors (NMFs), which help to keep it nourished.
● Put all the ingredients in a heatproof bowl and place in a saucepan half-filled with water.
● Gently heat until the honey and cocoa butter have dissolved and dispersed into the

plant oils. Stir to ensure all the ingredients have mixed thoroughly together.
● Pour into a small bottle or screw-top jar and give the mixture a final stir to prevent it from separating out as it sets.
● Apply at night, using light fingertip movements to pat around the entire eye area.

Luscious Lip Glosser

15 g (½ oz) beeswax pieces
25 g (1 oz) cocoa butter
25 ml (1 fl oz) castor oil
25 ml (1 fl oz) almond oil
8 drops clove essential oil

This lip balm moisturises, protects and shines the lips while also guarding against chapping and cold sores.

● Put the beeswax pieces, cocoa butter, castor oil and almond oil in a heatproof bowl and place in a saucepan half-filled with water. Heat gently until the beeswax and cocoa butter have melted. Remove from the heat and allow to cool, stirring continually.

● Add the drops of clove essential oil and pour into small glass jars. Tiny lip-gloss pots or clean make-up compacts are ideal. Place in the fridge to harden.

Dew-Drop Body Cream

120 ml (4 fl oz) almond oil
10 g (½ oz) beeswax pieces
50 g (2 oz) cocoa butter
350 ml (12 fl oz) herb tea
 (e.g. elderflower or
 rosehip)
8 drops lavender essential oil
 (optional)
100 g (4 oz) emulsifying
 ointment

This after-bath moisturiser encapsulates droplets of water that are absorbed by the skin as you rub it on. It is highly recommended as a regular treatment to keep the body sleek and smooth.

● Put the almond oil, beeswax pieces and cocoa butter in a heat-proof bowl and place in a saucepan half-filled with water. Alternatively microwave on High for 4 minutes.
● Gently heat until the beeswax and cocoa butter have completely dissolved. Remove from the heat and add the hot herb tea, lavender essential oil and emulsifying ointment, stirring continuously while the mixture cools.
● To make a stiffer moisturiser, use a little more emulsifying ointment and to make a lotion, use slightly less.

● Pour into a tub or large screw-top jar. Keep beside the bath or shower and massage liberally into the body after bathing.
● Instead of using the lavender oil you can fragrance this mixture with any essential oil according to personal preference. My own favourites for this recipe are sandalwood, coriander or neroli (orange blossom).

THE
ANTI-AGERS

As medical science gradually unravels the mysteries of skin ageing, so the cosmetic chemists are constantly trying to catch up with creams, serums and lotions that will help to turn back the clock. The last decade has without doubt been the age of the 'wrinkle removers' and we have been bombarded with creams from the cosmetic counters that promise much and cost even more. There is little doubt that some of these so-called miracle creams are a complete waste of money, but the cosmetic scientists have turned up some interesting findings that we can all use in everyday skincare.

HARMFUL SUN

For example, we now know that the sun is the skin's enemy number one. Unless we take steps to shield our faces from its glare our complexion quickly becomes wrinkly and slack almost as fast as a moisture-laden grape turns into a sun-dried raisin.

Not only do the sun's rays destroy the supporting collagen and elastin fibres of the face but they also encourage deep brown pigmentation marks known as 'age' or liver spots. The very best anti-ageing cream of all is a total sunblock, such as a simple zinc oxide cream, that protects the complexion from the damage the sun does to the lower levels of the skin. Protection is always far easier than a cure and it is well worth taking steps in our early years to ensure that our face never shows the ravages of premature sun-induced skin ageing.

But for those of us who spent our earlier years outdoors, or who plainly refuse to give up sunworshipping, there have been other skin-saving developments that can help keep the lines at bay. This chapter focuses on natural remedies that will actively help repair time-ravaged skin and give us the best chances of fighting the effects of skin ageing.

As highlighted in Natural Skin Science (see page 65), we now know that our skin responds to certain vitamins such as the antioxidants. This group of nutrients is sometimes referred to as the ACE vitamins, as it includes vitamin A (in the vegetable form of beta-carotene), vitamin C and vitamin E. In recent years antioxidants have become increasingly newsworthy as medical researchers discover that they can help many forms of chronic degenerative diseases such as cancer, coronary heart disease, cataracts and even signs of skin ageing.

Antioxidants work by protecting cells within the body from a kind of rusting process called oxidation. This occurs when cells come under attack from free radicals. Another modern medical buzz-word, free radicals are unstable particles that frequently occur within the body and cause a great deal of damage to our cells. Free radicals are on the increase because they are encouraged by factors of modern-day living such as chemical pollutants, smoking (including passive smoking) and the increased ultra-violet light that is slipping through our increasingly depleted ozone layer.

VALUABLE NUTRIENTS

In addition to the antioxidants there are several other types of nutrients that can ward off wrinkles. For example, the essential fatty acids are a group of important nutrients that help strengthen skin cells and keep them looking young. Found mainly in oily foods such as vegetable oils, avocados and oily fish, essential fatty acids are a valuable part of our diet as they act as internal moisturisers by strengthening skin cells from within. But the essential fatty acids and the antioxidant vitamins are not only important in our diet, they are also useful when applied directly to the surface of the skin. Beta-carotene and vitamin

E can penetrate the surface of the skin and it has also been clinically proven that some essential fatty acids help severe skin disorders when applied topically, as sometimes happens when evening primrose oil is rubbed on to patches of eczema.

Other scientific discoveries that help to slow down the formation of fine lines and wrinkles include the identification of certain fruit acids from plant extracts, the antioxidant properties of common herbs such as sage, parsley and thyme, and the powers of some essential oils to repair damaged skin. For example, sandalwood essential oil has been shown to stimulate skin cell growth. As highlighted on page 68, the new generation of skincare ingredients include herbal healers such as echinacea and gingko bilboa.

A HEALTHY GLOW

Although all these natural ingredients are important, other integral treatments to ward off wrinkles include exfoliation, exercise and massage. All three activities really do work because they boost the amount of blood brought to the surface of the skin, which carries with it fresh oxygen supplies. Oxygen is essential for healthy skin cell functioning and it is important to encourage sufficient supplies to reach the surface of the skin. Any form of exercise will benefit the complexion, even if it is only a brisk walk around the block. Massage also encourages increased blood flow to the skin's surface and is a wonderfully relaxing way of working out the face without moving a muscle.

Both exercise and massage also improve lymphatic drainage, which carries away toxins and cellular debris from beneath the surface of the skin. The lymphatic system runs parallel to the circulatory system throughout the body but, unlike the blood circulation, it does not have a heart to pump it around.

Instead, the lymphatic system relies on regular movements in the form of daily exercise or massage to keep it flowing smoothly. There is no doubt that by encouraging our lymphatic system to work harder we can quickly improve skin tone and luminosity — and literally wipe years off our faces.

Exfoliation also supports lymphatic drainage to a lesser extent, but has the added benefit of stimulating skin cell renewal. By gently buffing off dead cells from the skin's surface we automatically speed up the rate at which fresh, plump skin cells are produced to replace them. This in turn leads to clearer, smoother-looking skin.

In recent years we have learnt a great deal about the ways in which our skin ages and exactly what action is needed to slow down the signs of visible ageing. Using a sunblock is vital during the summer months and may even become essential during the winter, too, if our ozone layer continues to be depleted at the current rate. Diet is also a key factor in our over-all health and has a profound impact on our skin's appearance. By increasing our intake of fresh, unprocessed foods, such as whole grains, olive oil, fruits and vegetables that are rich in essential fatty acids and the antioxidant nutrients we can expect our skin to retain its youthful glow. Adding a daily exercise session, massage or exfoliation treatment is also important to help preserve long-term good looks. But, in addition to these guidelines, there are a few highly specific treatments that we can make to give our skin cells a boost and supply them with the ingredients our complexion needs to remain supple, healthy and strong.

Night-Time Nourishing Cream

25 g (I oz) cocoa butter
25 g (I oz) lanolin
25 ml (I fl oz) avocado oil
15 ml (I tbsp) wheatgerm oil
4 evening primrose oil capsules
10 drops neroli essential oil
10 drops frankincense essential oil

A wonderfully rich moisturiser that contains all the nutrients the skin needs to repair itself while we sleep. This soothing cream is also good for re-moisturising our hands, feet, elbows and legs.

● Put the cocoa butter and lanolin in a heatproof bowl and place inside a saucepan half-filled with water. Heat on top of the stove until the mixture has completely melted. Stir in the avocado oil, wheatgerm oil and contents of the evening primrose oil capsules (pierce with a pin).

● Remove from the heat and continually stir while the mixture cools. When the mixture has cooled to around body temperature, add the drops of essential oils and pour into small screw-top jars. Use as a nourishing night cream for the face and neck.

Skin Smoother

25 g (I oz) brewer's yeast powder
60 ml (4 tbsp) fresh apple juice
30 ml (2 tbsp) yogurt

The creamy texture of this gentle treatment is especially suited to mature, greying complexions in need of a boost. Brewer's yeast, which gives the cream its nutty scent, is our best natural source of the B-complex vitamins and is also rich in RNA (ribonucleic acid) and DNA (deoxyribonucleic acid), the basis of all living cells. Before each skin cell dies, DNA issues an order to RNA to reproduce itself. Therefore, our skin cells should reproduce themselves exactly as before. However, as our RNA and DNA break down in time the reproduction process also degenerates. Some studies show that external application of RNA and DNA, as brewer's yeast, may encourage skin cell rejuvenation.

● Dissolve the brewer's yeast powder in the apple juice (freshly pressed is best as it still retains useful levels of enzymes). Stir in the yogurt to form a smooth paste.

● Apply to freshly cleansed skin on the face and neck, leave for 15 minutes and rinse off thoroughly with plenty of tepid water. Follow with a layer of rich moisturiser.

Tired Eye Tonic

30 ml (2 tbsp) chamomile
    tea
30 ml (2 tbsp) witch hazel
5 ml (1 tsp) castor oil
2 drops frankincense
    essential oil

The perfect treatment for puffy
eyes, it leaves the delicate tissues around the eye area feeling
refreshed and smooth.

● Make the chamomile tea by
infusing 10 ml (2 tsp) of dried
chamomile flowers or 1 herb
tea bag with a cup of almost
boiling water. Allow to cool.
● Mix 30 ml (2 tbsp) of the
tea with the witch hazel and
pour into a screw-top jar. Add
the castor oil and 2 drops of
frankincense essential oil. Shake
the jar well to combine the
water-based extracts with the
castor oil.

● Dip several cotton wool pads
into the tonic, squeeze to
remove excess liquid and place
over the eye area. Alternatively,
apply to skin using a piece of
muslin cloth or clean face flannel. Leave in place for 10-15
minutes before removing.
● Store the remaining tonic in
the fridge (using chilled tonic
straight from the fridge is especially refreshing if eyes are sore
or puffy).

Fast-Acting Massage Oil

30 ml (2 tbsp) jojoba oil
30 ml (2 tbsp) wheatgerm
    oil
5 evening primrose oil
    capsules
3 drops frankincense
    essential oil

This is an ideal treatment to
use just before going to bed as
the oils are so rich they may
feel slightly sticky on the skin.

Leaving them on the face
overnight gives the blend time
to penetrate more deeply into
the skin and means you will
wake up with a softer,
smoother complexion.
● Blend the jojoba and wheatgerm oils together in a bowl or
screw-top jar. Pierce the
evening primrose oil capsules
with a pin and squeeze out the
contents into the mixture.

● Add the frankincense essential oil. Stir well to ensure all
the oils are mixed thoroughly.
● Using the tips of the fingers
only, massage into freshly
cleansed skin on the face and
neck. Use small circular movements to gently stimulate blood
flow and lymphatic drainage
just beneath the skin's surface.

Moisture Booster

½ small, very ripe avocado
1 egg yolk
5 ml (1 tsp) olive oil

This simple recipe gives the
skin an instant 'fix' of moisture
and is one of the easiest and
fastest to make.

● Mix together the ripe avocado, egg yolk and olive oil until
the ingredients combine to
form a smooth paste.
● Apply to clean skin on the
throat, neck and upper chest
area (you may find it easier to
use a large make-up brush or

pastry brush to paint the face
mask on to the skin). Relax for
15-20 minutes to give the
emollient ingredients sufficient
time to penetrate the upper levels of the skin.
● Remove with tissue or dampened cotton wool pads.

Echinacea Skin Soak

**150 ml (¼ pint) warm
  water**
20 drops echinacea tincture
**2 drops sandalwood essential
  oil**
**small muslin cloth or
  flannel**

This simple skin soak uses two of my favourite anti-ageing skincare ingredients. Herbal tinctures of echinacea are sold by most health shops, but try to find one that is not preserved in alcohol as this can occassionally irritate the skin.

This lotion also works well as a skin tonic and can be stored in a bottle and applied after cleansing on pads of cotton wool.

● Gently warm the water (bottled or filtered water is best for all skincare recipes) before adding the drops of echinacea tincture and the sandalwood essential oil.

● Soak the muslin cloth or flannel in the liquid, lightly wring and place over a freshly cleansed face and neck. Lie down and relax for 10-15 minutes. To seal in body heat, place a small hand-sized towel over the top, leaving a small gap for breathing.

● Remove and pat the skin dry, taking care not to wipe away any beneficial residues left on the skin.

Avocado Revitaliser

**½ small, very ripe avocado
  with skin and stone**
15 ml (I tbsp) yogurt
5 ml (I tsp) runny honey
**5 ml (I tsp) fresh lemon
  juice**

All parts of the avocado are used for this facial treatment. The action of rubbing the avocado stone over the skin stimulates pressure points on the face and boosts lymphatic drainage. It also increases blood circulation and gives the complexion an invigorating work-out.

● Remove the skin and stone from the halved avocado and set to one side.

● Mix the avocado flesh with the yogurt, runny honey and lemon juice until the mixture forms a smooth paste.

● Take the avocado skin and gently rub the inside part of the skin over the face and neck. This helps dislodge dead skin cells and prepares the skin for the revitalising face pack.

● Next, smooth the avocado mixture on to the face and throat, and relax for 10-15 minutes. Gently roll the avocado stone over the face and neck before rinsing the face mask away with warm water.

Linseed Tissue Toner

30 ml (2 tbsp) linseeds
60 ml (4 tbsp) hot water
2 drops cypress essential oil
   (optional)
piece of muslin cloth or
   cotton gauze

This treatment uses a warm linseed poultice to draw out excess fluid from puffy skin and firm up slackened skin tissues. Linseeds are rich in mucilages, which gently tighten and tone the skin, helping to leave it softer and smoother. The cypress essential oil is useful if you have broken veins. It acts as a vaso-dilator and as such, helps shrink broken blood capillaries, reducing their appearance.

● First, put the linseeds in a grinder and whizz for a few seconds, just to split open the seeds. Mix these with sufficient hot water to form a thick, gel-like paste. Add the cypress essential oil (if using) and stir thoroughly. Spread the mixture on to half the piece of muslin cloth or cotton gauze, folding the other half over to seal the poultice.

● Place over the lower half of the face and neck and leave for 10 minutes. To speed up the process, place a small towel over the top to seal in the heat.
● Hot linseed compresses also work well on specific areas of the face and body that need toning up. For example, a twice-weekly treatment on the chin and neck is an excellent way to help firm a double chin. Larger poultices can also be made and applied to areas of cellulite on the stomach, hips and thighs. These may be covered with clingfilm to intensify the process. Regular use, i.e. twice a week for at least a month, is important for best results.

Vitamin C Firming Lotion

2.5 g (½ tsp) ultra-fine
   vitamin C powder
45 ml (3 tbsp) glycerine and
   rosewater mixture

This lightly toning and moisturising lotion is enriched with vitamin C – renowned for its antioxidant restoring and firming effect on the skin. Vitamin C (also called ascorbic acid) is notoriously unstable in commercial skin creams. However, this method makes a little lotion at a time to ensure the nutrient actually stays active

when applied to the skin. The glycerine and rosewater mixture is available from chemists or may be made at home.
● Dissolve the vitamin C powder in the glycerine and rosewater. Pour a little of the mixture into an egg-cup or the palm of your hand and gently apply to your face and neck using your fingertips.
● This lotion can can also be applied to the backs of hands and the chest area. Follow with a moisturiser if needed.
● Store in a sealed, dark con-

tainer away from heat and light. The mixture should last for three or four days depending upon the quantity you use for each application. I also use this simple lotion on the backs of my hands to deter wrinkling and pigmented 'age' spots.

BATHS AND BODY CARE

The body is covered in an extremely large expanse of skin and yet, compared to our faces, it receives very little attention. Although the skin on the body spends most of its time under wraps, it has the same requirements for cleansing and moisturising as the face and neck. In fact, the body often needs more specialised care to treat specific problems such as severe dehydration, skin flaking, cellulite, water retention and areas of hardened, chapped skin. Fortunately, the treatments for such problems are often quick and simple, and most rely on natural plant and herbal ingredients for their active extracts. The only other equipment you need is a bath and/or shower to turn your home into a natural beauty salon.

HERBAL BATHS

The art of using herbal baths to treat skin and circulatory disorders is known as hydrotherapy. It is widely used on the Continent and many European health spas offer several types of healing baths to produce different effects within the body. These 'water cures' often involve special mineral waters or salt water from the sea. They may also be combined with mud or seaweed body treatments to boost the metabolism and stimulate the skin. There are an infinite number of possibilities when creating herbal baths, depending upon the herb extracts used and the temperature and volume of the water.

The best way to add herbal and plant extracts to bath water is to sew them inside a small muslin bag which can be dangled from the tap so the water releases a fresh infusion as it flows through it. A small cotton drawstring bag is also useful as it can be washed and re-used many times. You can also place herbs in a stocking foot and tie a knot in the leg. Alternatively, herb tea bags make a wonderfully simple addition to any bath and there are now several hundred varieties to choose from. Jacuzzis or whirlpool baths are also popular in health spas and beauty salons and are good to stimulate blood circulation and ease muscular stiffness. However, do not sit in a hot tub for more than ten minutes as it can make you feel faint and dizzy, and those with low blood pressure or heart problems should avoid them altogether.

Hot or Cold

At home, even something as basic as the temperature of the bath water is important. Warm baths are the most soothing as they help relax tense muscles and calm fragile nerves. These are also the best type to take after exercise as they help prevent stiffness in the joints and muscles. Therapeutically, warm baths are used to treat mild colds, urinary problems and low fevers. Both hot baths of temperatures of 38°C (100°F) or more and cold baths are essentially shock treatments for the body. Hot baths cause the pulse to increase and may leave you feeling weak and drained. Prolonged hot baths put the heart under unnecessary strain as the blood vessels expand in an attempt to cool the body. However, they can be useful to induce sweating and therefore good for eliminating toxins from the system. Cold baths also increase the rate at which the heart beats, although the pulse slows down once it has recovered from the initial shock. Cold baths can be especially helpful for boosting the blood circulation and toning the skin.

Few things are as relaxing as wallowing in a full bath and these are also the best for skin treatments as the entire body is submerged. Half-filled baths tend to be cooler and are less of a strain on the system, so better for those with low blood pressure. The sitz-bath (see page 113) is an Austrian invention and involves sitting in just a few inches of water. Many European health spas have specially designed sitz-baths, but you can use an ordinary bath and hang your legs over the side so that just your waist, bottom and upper thighs are covered by the water. Believe it or not, the best sitz-baths are taken cold — and once the body has recovered from the initial jolt it is amazing how quickly the condition of the skin improves. Although I am not especially brave, I try and take a quick cold dip at least two or three times a week as it really does get the blood circulation going.

The most minimal form of hydrotherapy is the footbath, which not only benefits the feet but can also invigorate the rest of the body depending on which herbal extracts are added to it. Over all, hydrotherapy has to be one of the easiest and most under-rated forms of health and beauty treatments, and it is well worth experimenting with some of the following variations.

Relaxing Baths

● To encourage a peaceful night, fill a muslin bag or sock with a dried herbal mixture designed to induce sleep and hang it under the hot tap. The herbs with most powerful sedative effects are valerian, lemon balm, marjoram, lavender, hops and passion flower. Alternatively, make a similar brew using herb tea bags and add to warm bath water.

● Add cold chamomile tea or two chamomile tea bags to a warm bath to help relax the muscles and delicately scent the skin.

● The following herbal mixture is useful for soothing strained muscles and relieving tension in the joints: infuse 5 ml (1 tsp) each of dried sage leaves, lavender flowers and chopped bay leaves in a cup of almost boiling water. Leave for 20 minutes. Strain then add the liquid to a pre-run warm bath.

● To soothe the skin and relax the mind, add 15 ml (1 tbsp) olive or peach kernel oil together with 6 drops of frankincense and 2 drops of chamomile essential oils to a warm bath.

● A few drops of essential oil transform an ordinary bath into a hedonistic indulgence. Amongst the most relaxing essences are lavender, melissa, sandalwood and bergamot. Always add the oils to a pre-run bath as they are broken down by heat and quickly loose their potency.

Invigorating Baths

● To stimulate the circulation and aid the digestion add a rosemary herbal infusion to the bath. Place 50 g (2 oz) fresh rosemary leaves and stalks in 600 ml (1 pint) of boiling water and leave to infuse for 15 minutes before pouring into the bath water.

● Adding peppermint to a cool bath is a traditional way of pepping up the body. Place dried peppermint inside a muslin sachet before adding to the bath water or simply add a handful of freshly chopped leaves and flowering tops. Leftover peppermint tea can also be saved and added to the bath.

• The most invigorating essential oils are the citrus oils such as lemon and mandarin, as well as rosemary, jasmine and peppermint (do not add more than a couple of drops of peppermint as its high menthol content can make the skin feel cold).

Moisturising Baths
• Take a tip from Cleopatra and her ass's milk by adding 15 ml (1 tbsp) dried milk powder to a pre-run warm bath to soften the skin while you soak.
• Make cotton sachets filled with finely ground oatmeal and place in the bath while the water is running. Use the sachet to gently scrub away dead and dingy skin cells from the upper arms, hips and thighs.
• Add 10 ml (2 tsp) olive oil or sunflower oil to the bath water just before stepping in. This leaves the skin feeling so soft that you won't need to use a body lotion afterwards. Take care when stepping in and out of the tub though, as this does make the sides of the bath quite slippery.

• Keep a jar of coconut oil in the bathroom and add a spoonful to each bath. For a more exotic skin treat, stir a few drops of rose or jasmine essential oil into the coconut oil. Just 3-4 drops will subtly scent a small jar of coconut oil and the scent lasts for ages.

HEALING HYDROTHERAPY
Water has been worshipped as a source of life since time began and sea water is renowned for its healing properties. It contains some sixty mineral salts and trace elements, most of which are essential to the human body. The Dead Sea in Israel is probably the most famous for its therapeutic properties, as it has the greatest concentration of salts and minerals. These are especially beneficial to those with psoriasis. Our own bath water may not be as nutritious, but by adding essential oils, mineral salts and other naturally active ingredients, it, too, possesses impressive healing powers.

Fast Footbaths
The footbath is a simple, straightforward treatment that can help a wide range of ailments. Ideally, the water should completely cover the feet and come halfway up the calves. Cold footbaths are good for reviving tired feet, and naturopaths often recommend them to ease headaches and insomnia. The feet should be submerged in the cold water for as long as possible or until the feet start to feel warm. Alternating between hot and cold footbaths is a time-honoured way to boost the blood circulation and can help prevent varicose veins in the legs. Feet and calves should first be placed in the hot footbath for two minutes, then plunged into cold water for one minute. This routine should be repeated ten times for maximum benefit.

Adding a few drops of lemon and peppermint essential oils to each footbath also helps to boost the blood flow and leaves the feet smelling fresh. Mustard footbaths are also a good way to ward off chilblains and help coughs and colds. Simply add 10 ml (2 tsp) strong English mustard to a hot footbath before soaking the feet for 15-20 minutes. Alternatively, add 15 ml (2 tsp) freshly grated ginger root to create a very effective, yet simple foot bath to help ward off colds and 'flu bugs.

The Sitz-Bath
As mentioned briefly at the beginning of this chapter, a cold sitz-bath is the most effective method of getting the circulation going. It is also specifically good for reducing haemorrhoids (piles) and for improving the appearance of varicose veins and small thread veins in the legs. Carried out regularly, a cold sitz-bath reduces signs of cellulite, improves the texture of the skin on buttocks and thighs and helps with weight loss by stimulating the metabolism. It is a wonderful treatment for those who sit still for most of the day as it prevents the blood from pooling in the lower half of the body. It is also a great way to revive the body after a stressful day's work.

A cold sitz-bath is quick, easy and not particularly painful: half-fill the bath with cold water (during the winter months a small amount of hot water may be added to ensure the water is not icy, but it is important that the water is cold — not lukewarm). Sit down in the bath bottom first, leaving your legs dangling over the side. The water should cover you from waist to upper thigh only. It makes the process far more pleasant if you leave your socks on to keep the feet warm and you can also wrap a towel or cardigan around the upper half of the body. Remain in the water for two minutes before getting out and briskly rubbing the skin dry. The sitz-bath takes almost no time at

all and can be carried out every day if desired. To see the maximum benefits it should be used at least three times a week.

A word of warning: the cold temperature may be too much of a shock to the system for anyone who is elderly, infirm or who has a cardio-vascular condition.

BATHTIME SKIN SAVERS
One of the most effective ways to treat skin conditions such as eczema and psoriasis is at bath time. Soaking in a bath containing oats or sea salts helps to soothe the skin and reduce inflammation. Baths can effectively calm, refresh or invigorate the skin depending upon the temperature of the water and what you add to them.

Eczema
To help soothe the itch and irritation of eczema, as well as psoriasis and dermatitis, make an oat bran decoction to add to the bath water. In a saucepan place 30 ml (2 tbsp) wheat bran with 30 ml (2 tbsp) oatmeal or porridge oat flakes and 600 ml

(I pint) water and gently bring to the boil. Remove from the heat and pass through a sieve. Add the milky liquid to a warm – not hot – bath, just before stepping in.

Psoriasis

Inflamed and itchy skin conditions can be relieved by adding sea water minerals to the bath water. The best come from the Dead Sea in Israel, where people with skin disorders go specifically to swim in its mineral-dense waters. Some health shops sell packets of sea water minerals from the Dead Sea to add to the bath, otherwise use two or three handfuls of sea salt combined with a few strips of dried culinary seaweed (the Clearspring brand can be found in most health shops, and wakame is a good variety to use) or 15 ml (I tbsp) kelp powder to re-create the effect.

Itchy Skin

Dry, sensitive skin is often caused when the skin's natural, acidic pH balance is disrupted. Avoid using soap in the bath (try the Simple Soapwort Cleanser on page 77) and add 15 ml (I tbsp) of cider vinegar to restore the correct acid/alkaline ratio. It is also worth adding a splash of aloe vera juice to help calm skin irritations.

Sunburn

The most important factor when treating sunburn is to cool the skin down quickly, to prevent the heat from penetrating the lower levels of the skin. Soaking in a deep, cool bath rapidly brings down body temperature and adding a handful of oatmeal or porridge oats also helps soothe angry, inflamed tissues. A few drops of lavender essential oil is also a wonderful skin soother and a natural antiseptic that works especially well on sunburned skin. Vitamin E in the form of

wheatgerm oil or from natural vitamin E capsules is also a useful addition to re-moisturise the skin and helps prevent peeling while reducing the risk of blisters.

SPA TIME

You don't need to spend a fortune on visiting a health farm when your body needs a bit of pampering. Many of the most effective spa treatments, such as body scrubs, mud packs and aromatherapy massage techniques are easy to carry out at home. Pick a quiet time at the weekend and take all the time you need to exfoliate, moisturise and massage your skin to reveal the new, fresh you.

Body Brushing

Dry skin brushing is one of the best all-round beauty treatments, and it can be carried out just before stepping into the bath or shower. It is a terrific treatment for dingy skin, cellulite and for improving a sluggish circulation. The best time to do dry skin brushing is first thing in the morning, just before bathing. You will need a natural-fibre body brush or massage mitt that feels firm, but not too harsh, on the skin. Starting with the soles of the feet, brush the legs from feet to thighs using strong, sweeping movements. Concentrate on the lymphatic drainage points located at the back of the knees and towards the groin, to increase the flow of lymph and assist the removal of toxins. Pay special attention to the backs of the thighs and buttocks to help break down fatty deposits from beneath the skin and reduce the appearance of cellulite. Carry on up the body, working gently over the stomach, sides and chest (avoiding the nipples). Brush up each arm, starting from the wrist and finishing on the upper inside arm.

Always brush towards the heart, as this is the way the lymph flows, and rinse the brush thoroughly after use. Dry skin brushing may feel strange and uncomfortable at first but it is well worth the effort. It increases the metabolism, improves skin tone, dislodges dingy skin cells and literally gets the whole body skin glowing (if you stand against the light while you brush you will see hundreds of dead skin cells flying off the body).

Body Scrubs
Other methods for improving the skin's texture and tone include body scrubs. These are best carried out either before or during a shower, as they tend to be quite a messy treatment. Body scrubs involve massaging the skin with a gritty substance to shift dead skin cells and embedded grime, and improve the appearance of spots and pimples. They can be used either on their own or in conjunction with a rough flannel or loofah to increase their effectiveness. Loofahs themselves are the long, fibrous pod of the *Luffa aegyptiaca* plant, which has been used as a body scrubber since Ancient Egyptian times. Massage pads and mitts can be made from pieces of loofah and these are good for scrubbing smaller areas of skin such as the hands and the soles of the feet. Loofahs should be kept clean by rinsing in clean water after each use and should be hung to dry to prevent them from becoming mouldy.

Basic Body Scrub

100 g (4 oz) granulated white sugar
100 g (4 oz) finely ground sea salt
100 g (4 oz) coarsely ground oatmeal

This simple mixture is made from ingredients found on most kitchen shelves, yet is just as effective as expensive skin exfoliators. The three ingredients work well together. Sugar is mildly anti-bacterial and helps heal minor skin irritations, the salt is an efficient body buffer, while the oatmeal soothes the skin as it gently dislodges dead skin cells.

● Mix the ingredients together in a large bowl and transfer to a screw-top jar. To use, pour a small amount into the palm of the hand and massage into dampened skin. Then rinse thoroughly.

● Keep the jar in the bathroom as the mixture is gentle enough to use each time you take a shower.

Peanut Butter Scrub

50 g (2 oz) crunchy peanut
    butter
25 g (1 oz) finely ground
    sea salt
30 ml (2 tbsp) almond oil

This body scrub tastes good
enough to eat! It is also rich in
natural oils that leave the skin
feeling fabulously soft and
smooth.

● Mix together the peanut butter with the sea salt and stir in
the almond oil. The mixture
should form a soft paste.
● Rub on to damp skin, all over
the body, concentrating on
areas of hard skin on the
elbows, upper arms and knees.
Rinse off with warm water and
shower as usual.

Extremely Gentle Bust Scrub

25 g (1oz) medium ground
    oatmeal
25 g (1 oz) finely ground
    almonds
15 ml (1 tbsp) almond oil

Most skin scrubs are too abrasive to use on the delicate skin
that covers the breasts, but a
gentle skin scrub is a good way
to preserve skin tone and to
remove any flakiness. The high
oil content leaves the skin
exceptionally smooth and will
enhance a tan.
● Mix together the oatmeal and
the almonds with the almond
oil to form a paste.
● Apply to dampened skin and
massage into the neck and chest
with firm but gentle circular
movements. Always massage
upwards to avoid pulling the
skin and encouraging slackening.
● Rinse thoroughly and shower
as usual. You will find the skin
is left feeling beautifully soft
and smooth.

Hip and Thigh Scrub

30 ml (2 tbsp) grapeseed oil
5 drops juniper essential oil
2 drops lemon essential oil
75 g (3 oz) polenta or
    cornmeal

This is my all-time favourite
body treatment as it is very
simple to do and really works
wonders on the skin. It is ideal
for shifting patches of stubborn
cellulite and should be carried
out at least twice a week to see
the best results. This is also an
ideal all-over treatment before a
shower and is usful as an anti-
ageing hand treatment to
remove flakiness, soften calluses
and leave the hands smooth.
● In a screw-top bottle or jar,
mix together the grapeseed oil
with the essential oils and shake
well. Pour over the cornmeal
and mix to form a gritty paste.
● Apply to dampened skin on
the hips, buttocks and thighs.
Massage firmly, using sweeping,
circular movements in an
upwards direction.
● For greater effect, use a rough
flannel or massage mitt instead
of the hands. Massage for at
least 2 minutes before rinsing
the gritty particles away. Rub
any leftover mixture into the
feet, hands and upper arms.

MUD, GLORIOUS MUD

Undoubtedly the messiest beauty treatment of all is the mud pack. It takes a real natural beauty enthusiast to try an all-over body pack, but the results are worth the extra effort. Mud packs work by using natural clays to draw out impurities, sebum and general grime from the pores of the skin. These clays also remove the top layer of dead skin cells, leaving the entire surface of the body soft, fresh and glowing. Mud packs may also be used for areas of acne on the back, or cellulite on the hips and thighs.

Whole-Body Mud Pack

150 g (5 oz) Fuller's earth
200 ml (7 fl oz) fresh apple
    juice
15 ml (1 tbsp) lemon juice
30 ml (2 tbsp) almond oil
15 ml (1 tbsp) runny honey
6 drops sandalwood or
    neroli essential oil

This all-over body treat is ideal just before a holiday, when you want your skin at its best, or as an annual 'spring clean' to invigorate grey, dingy skin. It is extremely effective, but be prepared for a mess!

● Mix together the Fuller's earth with the apple juice and lemon juice until it forms a smooth paste. Stir in the almond oil, honey and fragrant essential oil.

● To use, apply small amounts of the mixture to the body, starting at the feet and working upwards. Concentrate on areas of dull, dingy skin such as the hips, thighs and upper arms. Gently massage the mixture into the skin and leave for a few minutes to dry before stepping into the shower. Use warm water to thoroughly rinse away all traces of the mud pack, then shower as usual.

Anti-Acne Back Pack

2 egg whites, lightly beaten
100 g (4 oz) Fuller's earth
5 ml (1 tsp) alum crystals
5 ml (1 tsp) sulphur powder
6 drops tea tree essential oil

You will need a partner or close friend to help apply this properly, as most acne spots occur in hard to reach places in the middle of the back.
Any leftover mixture may be used on the feet to smooth and soften hard skin.

● Lightly beat the egg whites and mix with the Fuller's earth until they form a smooth paste (add a few drops of hot water if the mixture becomes too stiff to handle).

● Add the alum, sulphur and tea tree oil, mixing well.
● Ask a friend to massage the mixture into the back. Leave to dry completely. Shower with tepid water and pat dry.

MASSAGE OILS

The best follow-up to any type of body treatment is a gentle massage. The art of massage is the ultimate cure for stress, nervous tension and for promoting a feeling of well-being. There are two main reasons for using an oil while you massage. Firstly, an oil helps the hands glide over the skin and reduces friction. Secondly, the oil itself can be formulated to have moisturising and therapeutic properties. Massage oils made with natural plant oils are the best choice as they contain nourishing nutrients.

Basic Body Oil

120 ml (4 fl oz) grapeseed
  oil
5 ml (I tsp) wheatgerm oil
10 drops lavender or
  sandalwood essential oil

Excellent for everyday use, grapeseed oil has a light texture. If used sparingly, it won't leave sticky traces on clothes. It is a good idea to add wheatgerm oil which is rich in vitamin E and a natural antioxidant, and therefore prevents spoilage by rancidity.
● Mix the oils together and store in a screw-top bottle or jar. Shake before use.

Athlete's Muscle Rub

120 ml (4 fl oz) grapeseed
  oil
5 ml (I tsp) wheatgerm oil
10 drops rosemary essential
  oil
5 drops lavender essential oil
2 drops peppermint
  essential oil

This invigorating lotion is excellent for reviving a flagging physique and smells macho enough for the fussiest male!
● Mix the oils together in a screw-top bottle or jar.
● Shake well before use and apply liberally to areas of the body where the muscles have been working hardest, e.g. the calves, thighs and biceps.

Anti-Cellulite Oil

120 ml (4 fl oz) grapeseed
  oil
5 ml (I tsp) wheatgerm oil
10 drops juniper essential
  oil
5 drops lemon essential oil
5 drops fennel essential oil

This anti-cellulite formula is highly effective at breaking down the fatty deposits that lead to the dimpled, orange-peel effect on the thighs.

● Mix the oils in a screw-top jar and shake well before use.
● Use daily on the hips and buttocks after bathing, massaging into the skin, using firm, circular movements.

BODY LOTIONS

Body oils are good for massage but there are times when we may want to use a body lotion that sinks in more quickly and leaves a trace of delicate perfume on the skin.

Counter-Cellulite Thigh Cream

120 ml (4 fl oz) almond oil
10 g (½ oz) beeswax
50 g (2 oz) cocoa butter
720 ml (24 fl oz) water
5 g (⅛ oz) dried wakame seaweed
100 g (4 oz) emulsifying ointment
10 drops juniper essential oil
2 capsules powdered gingko biloba

This richly nourishing body lotion contains, in my opinion, the most effective natural ingredients to stimulate the removal of toxins that contribute to the build-up of dreaded cellulite.

● Put the almond oil, beeswax and cocoa butter into a heat-proof bowl and place in a saucepan half-filled with water. Heat gently until the beeswax and cocoa butter have completely dissolved. Alternatively, microwave on 'High' for 4 minutes.

● Meanwhile, chop the seaweed. Put in a pan with the water, bring to the boil, then steep for 15 minutes. Strain.
● Add the hot seaweed infusion, gingko biloba, juniper oil and emulsifying ointment to the almond oil mixture, stirring until cool. Pour into a screw-top jar and massage into problem cellulite areas daily after bathing.

Rose Petal Body Lotion

15 g (½ oz) anhydrous lanolin
15 g (½ oz) cocoa butter
20 ml (4 tsp) almond oil
20 ml (4 tsp) glycerine (preferably vegetable)
6 drops rose essential oil

This richly moisturising cream smells delicious and is a won-derful treatment for areas of parched, chapped skin.
● Put the lanolin and cocoa butter in a heatproof bowl and place in a saucepan half-filled with water. Heat gently until melted and the mixture forms a smooth paste. Remove from the heat and stir in the almond oil and glycerine (use vegetable glycerine if you prefer a cruelty-free, vegetarian cream).
● Allow to cool before adding the rose essential oil, stirring well (rosewood or rose geranium essential oils are good alternatives to expensive pure rose oil). Pour the mixture into a small jar and apply liberally to dry skin after bathing.

HAND AND FOOT CARE

Hands and feet are our hard-working extremities and deserve pampering with a little extra care and attention. The skin that covers our hands and feet is much thicker than elsewhere on the body. This provides them with important protection during their arduous daily tasks, but can sometimes result in a build-up of rough, chapped skin that looks unsightly and is often painful. Our hands especially are always out on constant show and are continually exposed to the elements. Strong sunshine encourages brown 'age' spots on the backs of the hands, cold weather leaves them dry and chapped, while washing in soapy water strips away their natural oils, leaving them rough and wrinkled.

Our feet come under a different kind of pressure as they carry our weight around all day, often squeezed into tightly-fitted boots and shoes. During the winter months the skin on our feet may go for months without being allowed to breathe properly, as feet are cocooned in constant layers of thick tights, woolly socks and warm bedclothes. It is said that the expression on your face is due to the comfort of your feet and it is certainly true that corns, chilblains and bunions cause a great deal of misery. So it is hardly surprising that pedicures have become one of the most popular beauty treatments – a small amount of time spent looking after the feet can put a smile on the face all year round.

Finger-nails and toe-nails also require regular care to keep them trim and attractive.

Giving yourself a weekly manicure and pedicure is a simple beauty treatment that keeps nails tidy and prevents problems such as splitting, flaking and painful in-growing toenails. In between treatments, follow this seven-point plan to healthier hands.

● Always wear a pair of gloves or use a barrier cream when outside or doing chores such as gardening or the washing-up.

● Avoid plunging the hands into too-hot or freezing-cold water as this encourages dehydration and leads to skin chapping.

● Always use a sunblock when out in sunny weather to prevent the formation of brown 'age' spots on the backs of the hands.

● Get into the habit of using a rich hand cream last thing at night.

● Include vegetable oils in your daily diet, such as olive or sunflower oils for cooking, or food supplements such as cod liver oil or evening primrose oil to help strengthen weak, brittle nails.

● Always trim hang-nails to prevent them tearing or splitting.

● Avoid opening the mail, cans, jars, etc. with the nails as this weakens the structure and encourages them to break off.

The following remedies are easy to make and are well worth including in your regular beauty routine. Not only do they make the hands and feet look more attractive, but they also help prevent more serious disorders from developing in the future.

Lavender Barrier Cream

10 g (¼ oz) beeswax pieces
25 g (1 oz) cocoa butter
60 ml (4 tbsp) almond oil
15 ml (1 tbsp) castor oil
15 drops lavender essential
   oil

This waterproof hand cream will protect the hands from environmental abuse and is perfect to use before chores such as gardening and washing-up.

Keep a tub handy in the kitchen for regular use. Instead of using lavender essential oil, the cream may also be scented with lemon or sandalwood oils for a more macho aroma.

● Put the beeswax pieces and cocoa butter in a heatproof bowl and place in a saucepan half-filled with water. Gently heat until the beeswax and cocoa butter have melted together. Remove from the heat and stir in the almond oil and castor oil.

● Allow to cool and beat in the lavender essential oil. Pour the mixture into tubs or shallow screw-top jars and rub into the hands whenever a protective barrier cream is needed.

Cuticle Cream

10 g (¼ oz) beeswax pieces
60 ml (4 tbsp) almond oil
5 drops lavender essential oil
10 drops tea tree essential
   oil

This nourishing cream also contains essential oils to heal minor skin irritations and the inclusion of the tea tree essential oil will help prevent common fungal nail infections.

● Put the beeswax pieces and almond oil together in a heatproof bowl and place in a saucepan half-filled with water. Gently heat until the beeswax has completely melted into the oil. Stir thoroughly, remove from the heat and allow to cool slightly. Then stir in the essential oils.

● Pour the mixture into a small screw-top jar and use to massage daily around the nails to soften cuticles and prevent them from splitting and peeling.

Hot Oil Smoother

50 ml (2 fl oz) almond oil
20 ml (4 tsp) wheatgerm oil
10 drops lavender essential
   oil
pair of old cotton socks
pair of cotton gloves

This is an excellent overnight intensive treatment for re-moisturising hard skin on the hands and feet. The hot oil rapidly soaks into the upper layers of skin and is sealed in with cotton socks and gloves. This encourages our natural body heat to boost penetration of the oil even further (cotton manicure gloves are available from major department stores and some chemists).

● Warm the almond oil in a small saucepan. Add the wheatgerm oil and lavender essential oil and remove from the heat.

● Apply liberally to clean feet and hands, massaging well into the skin before covering with cotton socks and gloves. Leave overnight and in the morning the skin will feel fabulously soft and smooth.

Orange Blossom Massage Cream

5 ml (I tsp) lecithin
   granules, or 4 lecithin
   capsules
25 ml (I fl oz) rosewater
25 ml (I fl oz) almond oil
50 ml (2 fl oz) olive or
   avocado oil
10 g (¼ oz) beeswax pieces
20 drops neroli or petitgrain
   essential oil

Pure neroli essential oil gives
this cream its luxurious orange
blossom scent, but less expensive alternatives include petitgrain, bergamot or ylang ylang
oils. This moisturising mixture
also makes a good massage
balm and skin salve.

● Put the lecithin granules or
the contents of the capsules to
soak in the rosewater for several
hours, preferably overnight. Put
the almond oil, olive or avocado oil and beeswax pieces in a
heatproof bowl and place in a
saucepan half-filled with water.

● Gently heat until the beeswax
has melted completely. Add the
lecithin and rosewater, and beat
vigorously before removing
from the heat.
Add the essential oil of your
choice to fragrance the cream.

● Allow to cool slightly before
pouring into a shallow tub or
screw-top jar (scraping the
cream from the sides of the
mixing bowl before it sets). To
use, massage liberally into
rough, chapped skin on the
hands, elbows and feet.

Athlete's Foot Bath

1 small onion
1 clove garlic
1 cm ($\frac{1}{2}$ inch) fresh ginger
  root
25 g (1 oz) dried sage
25 g (1 oz) dried rosemary
3.4 litres (6 pints) hot water
20 drops tea tree essential
  oil

This footbath treats fungal infections of the foot and is also invigorating for feet that are sore and tired from strenuous exercise such as step-aerobics, running or skiing.

● Chop the onion and garlic, and finely grate the ginger root. In a large saucepan, make a herbal infusion by adding the onion, garlic, ginger root and herbs to the hot water.
● Gently simmer for 5 minutes before removing from the heat and leaving to steep for 10 more minutes. Strain the liquid and allow to cool slightly.

● Add the tea tree essential oil and pour into a large bowl.
● Soak the feet for 20 minutes, covering with a towel to prevent the heat from escaping. Then pat every part of the foot dry, especially in-between the toes.
● Finish with a light dusting of medicated talcum powder or arrowroot that has been infused with the scent from a few whole juniper berries.

Hard-Skin Remover

50 g (2 oz) cocoa butter
50 g (2 oz) polenta or
  cornmeal
25 g (1 oz) Fuller's earth
10 drops lemon or mandarin
  essential oil

This treatment is ideal for buffing away calluses that have formed on the hands or feet, or for smoothing pimply patches on elbows or knees.

● In a small saucepan gently melt the cocoa butter. Remove from the heat and stir in the polenta and Fuller's earth until the mixture forms a thick paste. Beat in the essential oil.

● To use, massage into areas of rough skin on the feet, hands, elbows and knees. Use firm, circular movements to help shift calluses and leave the skin feeling silky smooth. Wipe away excess cream with a warm, damp cloth or flannel. Follow with an application of Orange Blossom Massage Cream (page 124).

At-Home Manicure

nail polish remover
cotton wool pads
nail scissors
emery board or nail file
Cuticle Cream (page 123)
rubber hoof stick
orange sticks
Orange Blossom Massage
   Cream (page 124)

Regular manicures are one of the easiest beauty salon treatments to carry out at home and will make all the difference to the long-term state of our hands and nails. Aim to give the hands a weekly manicure.

● Wash hands and nails in warm, soapy water and dry thoroughly.

● Remove any nail polish with remover on cotton wool pads.

● Trim long nails with nail scissors and file into a smooth oval shape, using an emery board or non-metal nail file.

Avoid 'sawing' backwards and forwards as this weakens the nail. The best way to file the nails is in one direction only.

● After filing, rinse the fingertips in warm water and pat dry.

● Apply a small amount of Cuticle Cream around each nail and massage into the cuticle and base of the nail. Leave for a few minutes for the cream to penetrate and soften the skin.

● Next, take the rubber hoof stick and gently push back the cuticle from around each nail. Never force the skin back and avoid cutting or poking the cuticle as this can pierce the skin and lead to infections. When you have been around each cuticle, take an orange stick and wipe around the base of each nail to remove traces of cuticle cream.

● Apply a generous dollop of Orange Blossom Massage Cream and work into the fingers, palms and wrists. Each hand contains twenty-eight small bones and a complex network of muscles and tendons, so spend at least 10 minutes giving the hands a gentle massage. This not only releases tension and loosens up stiff joints but also increases blood circulation and keeps the skin feeling supple and smooth.

At-Home Pedicure

nail polish remover
cotton wool pads
footbath or washing-up
   bowl
stiff nail brush
soap or Soapwort Cleanser
   (page 77)
small towel
nail scissors
emery board or nail file
Cuticle Cream (page 123)
rubber hoof stick
cuticle clippers
Orange Blossom Massage
   Cream (page 124)
talcum powder

Aim to give your feet a pedicure at least once a month to keep calluses, corns and bunions at bay.

● Begin by removing any nail polish from the toenails with remover and cotton wool pads.
● Half-fill the footbath or washing-up bowl with warm water and soak the feet for at least 5 minutes to allow the skin to warm and soften.
● Gently scrub the feet and toes with a stiff nail brush and soap or Simple Soapwort Cleanser.
● Dry the feet and toes thoroughly and trim long nails by cutting straight across with a small pair of nail scissors.
● Smooth any rough edges of the nails with an emery board or non-metal nail file.
● Apply a small amount of Cuticle Cream to each toenail and massage into the cuticles.
● Use a rubber hoof stick to gently encourage the cuticles

away from the nail bed, but be careful not to jab or poke too vigorously as this can pierce the skin and lead to infections. Use a sharp pair of cuticle clippers to cut away any small pieces of dead cuticle, but take care not to snip any living tissue.
● Spend the next 10 minutes massaging the feet with a generous helping of Orange Blossom Massage Cream – you will be rewarded for your efforts afterwards when your feet feel as though they are walking on air.
● Finally, dust in between the toes with talcum powder (you can make your own by mixing together equal quantities of arrowroot and cornflour, scented with small pieces of chopped orange and lemon peel).

In between treatments you can encourage healthy feet, ankles and toes by following these six steps to healthier feet.
● Switch heel heights during the day to give the feet and calves a break. If you wear high heels during the day, slip into a pair of pumps in the evening.
● Invest in a corrugated foot roller to give the feet a reflexology-style work-out during the day. Simply move the feet along

the roller to stimulate the nerve endings on the soles of the feet.
● Use a rich moisture cream on your feet at night and wake up to softer toes.
● Always wear well-fitting shoes and have your feet professionally measured from time to time when choosing a new pair, in case of change.
● Apply a daily dab of Cuticle Cream or almond oil to the toenails to keep cuticles soft

and well conditioned.
● Always trim toenails straight across, never down at the sides, to prevent in-growing toenails.

HERBAL
HAIR CARE

Hair consists of a type of protein called keratin, which responds well to many beauty treatments. Keratin itself is a peculiar horny substance that also makes up our nails, and even the horns of wild animals. It is pushed out from hair follicles that cover the scalp and grows into long strands. Each hair strand has a central cortex which is soft and a coating of hard scales on the outside which are the cuticles. As with our skin, the hair is moisturised by the body's own protective oil called sebum. This is secreted from sebaceous glands in the scalp and travels along each hair strand to coat the cuticles, keeping them shiny and smooth. Unfortunately, many factors interfere with the health of our scalp and hair. Diet is important as the hair follicles rely on a steady stream of nutrients delivered daily by the blood supply.

The most important nutrients for healthy hair are vitamins A, B-complex, C and D, together with zinc, iron and the essential fatty acids found mainly in vegetable oils. Other lifestyle factors that interfere with a healthy head of hair include smoking, excess alcohol, not taking enough exercise and too much stress. Our hormones also play an important part in the condition of our hair and can affect hair loss and scalp disorders such as dandruff. Most of the other problems that occur are inflicted by ourselves. Washing in harsh detergent-based shampoos, over-heating with hot hairdryers, curling tongs and heated rollers, or over-brushing and back-combing all conspire to reduce our hair to a mass of dry tangles.

The basic rules of effective hair care are simple and will dramatically improve the condition of all hair types.

● Wash hair gently in a mild shampoo. Vigorous scrubbing can stimulate the sebaceous glands to producing excess sebum and lead to greasy hair.

● Hair should be washed every other day or possibly once a day, if you live in a polluted, urban environment.

● Avoid using too much shampoo, which can strip away the scalp's naturally protective oils. One shampooing should be sufficient, unless your hair is full of styling products such as sticky lacquer or hair gel.

● All hair types will benefit from a light conditioner to protect the scales on the hair cuticle and encourage a glossy shine.

● Turn down the setting on your hairdryer to avoid over-heating the hair. This is especially important if your hair has been chemically treated with colourants or a perm. Ideally, let your hair dry naturally once in a while.

● Treat your hair to a weekly scalp massage which will encourage fresh blood supplies to flow to the surface of the scalp and feed the hair follicles.

● Dry and chemically damaged hair should be given an intensive moisturising treatment once a week.

Hair should be our crowning glory and it is easy to coax it into better condition with these herbal hair care recipes.

Sandalwood and Soapwort Shampoo

25 g (1 oz) chopped
  soapwort root
25 g (1 oz) dried chamomile
  flowers
250 ml (8 fl oz) hot water
20 drops sandalwood
  essential oil

This simple shampoo is gentle
on the skin and suitable for all
hair types. Although soapwort
root is an efficient cleanser, it
does not produce a lather like
conventional detergent-based
shampoos.

● Place the chopped soapwort
root and chamomile flowers in
a bowl and pour on the almost-
boiling water. Stir well, cover
and leave overnight to infuse.

● In the morning, strain the
liquid and add the drops of the
sandalwood essential oil.
● To use, wet the hair and massage in a small amount of the
mixture. Rinse and repeat.

No-Wash Shampoo

50 g (2 oz) powdered orris
  root
25 g (1 oz) semolina or
  ground rice
10 drops lemon essential oil
10 drops neroli essential oil

This is a useful way of cleaning
the hair when you can't or don't
want to wash it with water. The
method of dry-hair shampooing
works best on short and
medium-length hair and absorbs
dirt, sebum and general grime
from the hair and scalp.

● In a large bowl mix the orris
root and semolina or ground
rice together. Sprinkle in the
drops of essential oil and stir
the mixture to distribute the
fragrance. Transfer to a screw-
top jar for storage.
● To use, tip the head upside-
down and brush the hair forward. Rub small amounts of
the mixture into the scalp,
starting at the base of the neck
and working forward.

● Use a natural bristle brush to
brush the hair thoroughly,
working the mixture through
the hair from the roots to the
ends. Throw the head back and
brush out any remaining particles of mixture. The hair will
be left feeling clean, soft and
fragrant.

Dry Hair and Scalp Shampoo

25 g (I oz) chopped
   soapwort root
500 ml (17 fl oz) hot water
25 g (I oz) coconut oil
15 drops sandalwood or
   patchouli essential oil

This shampoo gently re-mois-
turises the hair and scalp.
Note that the soapwort root
has excellent cleansing properties but does not produce much
lather. This shampoo is mild
enough to be used on children
and babies, but use chamomile
essential oil for the fragrance as
this is gentler on their scalps
and avoid the eyes.

● Add the chopped soapwort
root to the hot water, cover and
leave to infuse overnight. In the
morning, remove the pieces of
root and strain the liquid.

● In a small saucepan, gently
melt the coconut oil and add
to the soapwort decoction. Stir
in the drops of essential oil to
subtly fragrance the shampoo.
● To use, massage a small
amount of the pre-warmed
mixture into the scalp and rinse
with plenty of hot water.

Cleansing Clay Shampoo

100 g (4 oz) coconut oil
100 g (4 oz) Fuller's earth
120 ml (4 fl oz) chamomile
   tea
30 ml (2 tbsp) cider vinegar
10 drops peppermint
   essential oil

This unusual shampoo is especially good for removing flakes
of dead skin from the scalp and
for absorbing excess sebum.
The peppermint oil also makes
the shampoo feel refreshing on
the skin and boosts the blood
to the scalp.

● Place the coconut oil in a
small bowl and stir in the
Fuller's earth powder. Set to
one side while you make the
chamomile tea by infusing 10
ml (2 tsp) of dried chamomile
flowers, or I chamomile herb
tea bag, in a cupful of almost-
boiling water. Leave to steep
for 5 minutes before straining.
● Beat in 120 ml (4 fl oz) of
chamomile tea and the cider
vinegar, and transfer to a large,
shallow tub or jar.

● To use, rub small amounts of
the mixture into the scalp, massaging gently to dislodge dead
skin cells. Leave for 5 minutes
before rinsing thoroughly with
plenty of warm water. As this
cleansing treatment removes
excess oil from the scalp and
hair shafts, it should be followed with a light conditioner.

Aromatic Pomade

50 ml (2 fl oz) almond oil
25 ml (1 fl oz) castor oil
20 drops neroli essential oil
10 drops lavender essential
   oil
10 drops lemon essential oil

This natural hair shiner is based on a Renaissance recipe, when fragrant oils were popular with noblemen and women to keep their hair smelling sweet.

● In a screw-top bottle or jar, mix together the almond and castor oils. Add the aromatic essential oils and shake well.

● To use, apply a few drops to the fingertips and massage into the hair, or rub a few drops on the bristles of a hairbrush and brush through the hair. This wonderfully fragrant mixture leaves the hair subtly scented, and with a healthy, glossy shine.

Styling Lotion

50 g (2 oz) sugar
250 ml (8 fl oz) boiling
   water
30 ml (2 tbsp) flat beer
15 drops lemon or neroli
   essential oil

This traditional hair-styling lotion was popular during the war years when conventional setting lotions were not so readily available.

● Dissolve the sugar in the boiling water and leave to cool. Add the beer and essential oil (this is important to avoid smelling like a brewery).

● Apply to wet or damp hair after shampooing and use to set the hair on rollers or with curling tongs. Leftover liquid can be kept in a plastic spray bottle and used in between washes when re-styling the hair.

Dry-Ends Cream

50 g (2 oz) coconut oil
50 g (2 oz) cocoa butter
30 ml (2 tbsp) almond oil
15 drops neroli essential oil

Although nothing mends split ends once they have broken, this mixture temporarily seals them and discourages the hair shaft from splitting further.

● In a small saucepan melt together the coconut oil with the cocoa butter. Remove from the heat and stir in the almond oil. When the mixture has cooled slightly add the neroli essential oil.

● To use, rub a small amount between the fingertips and apply sparingly to dry hair ends in between washes. This mixture may also be used as an intensive hair-conditioning treatment before shampooing. Simply massage into the hair and scalp, cover the head with a towel to seal in body heat and leave for 20 minutes before shampooing out.

Intensive Hair Conditioner

15 ml (1 tbsp) black strap
  molasses
2 egg yolks
50 ml (2 fl oz) avocado or
  almond oil

This unconventional hair conditioner is a rich, dark, deeply nutritious liquid which works well on dry, chemically processed hair as it leaves the hair strands unusually shiny and smooth.

● In a small bowl, vigorously beat together the molasses and egg yolks until they form a stiff paste. Add the avocado or almond oil and mix again.

● Apply to dry hair, working through the ends of the hair up towards the roots.
● Leave for 15-20 minutes and wash the hair as usual, using two applications of shampoo to remove all traces of the conditioner.

Sesame Sun-Screener

50 ml (2 fl oz) sesame oil
25 g (1 oz) coconut oil
10 ml (2 tsp) wheatgerm oil

The sesame oil in this formula shields the hair from about a third of the sun's damaging ultra-violet rays. This emollient hair sunscreen also acts as an intensive conditioner and prevents the hair from drying out in the sun. It is especially good for dry, tinted or permed hair, which is more porous than most and therefore prone to sun damage.

● Place the sesame oil and coconut oil in a small saucepan and heat gently until the coconut oil has melted. Remove from the heat and stir in the wheatgerm oil.
● Pour into a small bottle or jar and shake well before use. Apply by combing through dry hair just before you go out sunbathing.

Hot-Oil Hair Restructuriser

50 ml (2 fl oz) olive oil
10 drops sandalwood
  essential oil

This treatment is especially good for dry, tinted or permed hair which has become brittle and unmanageable.

● Gently warm the olive oil in a small saucepan. Add the drops of sandalwood essential oil and stir thoroughly.
● Apply to dry hair and comb through from the roots to the ends using a wide-toothed comb. Massage any remaining oil gently into the scalp.

● Wrap the hair and scalp in a towel, turban-style, to seal in the body heat from the scalp. Leave for 20 minutes before shampooing twice with a mild shampoo.

Cradle Cap Treatment

50 ml (2 fl oz) almond oil
50 ml (2 fl oz) calendula oil
10 drops chamomile
   essential oil

Cradle cap is a common scalp complaint during infancy and is easy to improve with this gentle treatment. The oils are extremely soothing on a baby's fragile scalp.

● Mix together the almond and calendula oils and add the chamomile essential oil. Store in a screw-top bottle or jar and shake vigorously before use.

● To use, massage a small amount into the affected area before bathing. Lightly shampoo using a mild, baby shampoo and pat the scalp dry.

● For severe cases, a few drops may be rubbed into the affected area in between hair washes.

Re-Moisturising Scalp Lotion

50 ml (2 fl oz) avocado oil
50 ml (2 fl oz) almond oil
25 ml (1 fl oz) cider vinegar
30 ml (2 tbsp) strong nettle
   tea
10 drops peppermint
   essential oil
10 drops lavender essential
   oil

A good treatment for itchy, flaky scalps, or for those prone to thinning hair.

● Measure the avocado and almond oils into a screw-top bottle or jar. Add the cider vinegar and shake well.

● Make the nettle tea by infusing 10 ml (2 tsp) of nettle leaves in 120 ml (4 fl oz) of almost-boiling water.

● Leave to steep for 10 minutes, strain and add 30 ml (2 tbsp) to the oil and vinegar mixture. Shake vigorously to emulsify the liquid.

● When cool, add the peppermint and lavender essential oils. To use, shake the bottle and rub a small amount daily into the scalp by parting the hair and applying with cotton wool.

NATURAL HAIR RINSES

Herbal hair rinses are an ideal way to follow your final shampoo. Based on natural ingredients, they help restore the correct pH balance to the hair and scalp. Hair rinses also remove the mineral deposits left on the hair by hard-water washing, and encourage a glossy shine.

Normal hair
● Fresh elderberries make a fantastic hair shiner. Simmer with water for 15-20 minutes before straining off the juice. Apply to the hair before washing, leave for 15 minutes then shampoo as normal.
● Adding 5 ml (1 tsp) of cider vinegar to your final rinsing water is also a good way to restore the correct pH balance and leave the hair gleaming.

Dry and chemically processed hair
● This can be further dried by hard water so make your own soft water rinse by adding 5 ml (1 tsp) of domestic borax to 3.4 litres (6 pints) of warm water.
● You may also add 5 ml (1 tsp) of cider vinegar to restore pH balance and 6 drops of chamomile essential oil to fragrance the hair.

Oily hair
● Make a herbal infusion based on 15 ml (1 tbsp) of chopped fresh mint leaves, 15 ml (1 tbsp) of chopped fresh rosemary leaves, and the juice of 1 lemon mixed with 300 ml (½ pint) of hot water. Leave to infuse for 15 minutes, strain and use as a final hair rinse.

Lank or limp hair
● Make a herbal infusion with 15 ml (1 tbsp) chopped fresh rosemary mixed with 250 ml (8 fl oz) hot water. Leave to steep for 15 minutes, strain and add the juice of 1 lemon and 30 ml (2 tbsp) of flat beer. Mix well and apply to the hair as a final rinse after shampooing.

Blonde hair
● Use the freshly squeezed juice of 2 lemons mixed with an equal quantity of water. Comb through wet hair after shampooing and leave for 15-20 minutes before rinsing.
● Add 100 g (4 oz) of dried chamomile flowers to 500 ml (17 fl oz) of almost-boiling water. Leave to infuse for 30 minutes and use as a final rinse to bring out naturally blonde highlights in the hair.
● A pinch of saffron infused in hot water will also make a good finishing rinse to bring out a darker shade of blonde.

Brunette hair
● Infuse 4 sticks of dried cinnamon in 100 ml (3½ fl oz) of boiling water. Leave to cool before using on freshly washed hair to leave a trace of spice-shaded highlights.

Dark hair
● Make an infusion based on 25 g (1 oz) of sage leaves in 3.4 litres (6 pints) of almost-boiling water. Steep for 2 hours. Leave on the hair for 30 minutes before rinsing out.
● Mix 1 cup of strong black coffee with the freshly squeezed juice of 1 lemon. Leave on the hair for 30 minutes after shampooing before rinsing out.

Red hair
● Save the cooking water from beetroots to use as a natural plum-coloured hair dye. Use sparingly and wear rubber gloves or you will end up with purple fingers too!
● Use a glass of red wine as a final rinse to bring out naturally auburn highlights.

Anti-Itch Scalp Rinse

500 ml (17 fl oz) nettle tea
30 ml (2 tbsp) cider vinegar
6 drops chamomile essential
oil

This is a useful final hair rinse to soothe dry, flaky scalps.

● Make the nettle tea by infusing 50 g (2 oz) of fresh, young nettle tops in 500 ml (17 fl oz) of almost-boiling water. Alternatively, use 20 ml (4 tsp) of dried nettles or 2 nettle herb tea bags. Allow to steep for 10 minutes before straining.

● Add the cider vinegar and chamomile essential oil and stir well to mix.
● Pour over the scalp after the final rinse and massage gently into the skin. Do not rinse out. Repeat three times a week.

Anti-Dandruff Hair Tonic

1.2 litres (2 pints) strong
nettle tea
250 ml (8 fl oz) birch
infusion

While it is usual for the scalp to shed dead skin cells, dandruff is a scalp condition that occurs when the surface skin cells grow faster than normal, resulting in a build-up of scurf on the scalp. Dry, itching scalps may be caused by an allergic reaction to your shampoo, or simply by the scalp drying out. Investing in a small humidifier for your home or office may also be useful.

Nettles contain many beneficial minerals, including iron and zinc, and both nettles and birch have been used by herbalists since Roman times to treat scalp disorders.

● To make the tonic, simmer a handful of young nettle tops in 1.2 litres (2 pints) water for 2 hours. Alternatively, make a strong nettle tea using 45 ml (3 tbsp) of dried nettle leaves or 4 nettle herb tea bags.
● While the nettle tea is infusing, make the birch infusion by stirring 15 ml (1 tbsp) fresh or dried birch leaves into a cupful of almost-boiling water. Leave to steep for 30 minutes.

● When the two infusions are ready, mix together, strain and pour into bottles. Apply to the hair and scalp 2-3 times a week, or use as a final hair rinse after washing. Do not rinse out.

GLOSSARY

Anti-inflammatory

This is a substance that reduces inflammation of the tissues, so reducing pain and swelling. Some anti-inflammatory plant extracts contain substances that are similar to steroids, such as marigold and liquorice. Others contain painkilling ingredients similar to aspirin; for example, Balm of Gilead and willowbark (from which aspirin was first extracted). Anti-inflammatory plants such as dandelion and marigold, and citrus oils may also work by stimulating the circulation.

Antioxidant

An antioxidant is a substance that prevents the formation of destructive free radicals within the body and skin. Natural antioxidants include vitamins C and E and beta-carotene, which also act as preservatives in skincare recipes.

Antiseptic

Many plants have antiseptic properties, meaning they fight infections and germs on the surface of the skin. Most essential oils are antiseptic, and plants containing high levels of tannins are also antiseptic. Others, such as marigold, thyme and tea tree, also have anti-fungal effects.

Anti-spasmodic

This is a term given to herbs or other substances that prevent or relieve spasms within the body.

Aromatherapy

This is the therapeutic use of essential oils to treat many disorders, notably skin complaints, cellulite, hormonal problems and stress.

Astringent

An astringent is any substance that causes the contraction of body tissue. In skincare it is a term given to liquids that temporarily tighten the skin. In herbalism, plants with astringent properties work by binding protein molecules together to provide a protective surface on the delicate areas such as mucous membranes, to prevent inflammation and aid healing. Astringent plants tend to have a high tannin content.

Carrier Oils

Vegetable oils are used in aromatherapy to carry the more concentrated essential oils on to the skin. Carrier oils include almond and grapeseed oils.

Decoction

This is a liquid made by pouring cold water on to finely chopped plant material and simmering. The process is used to extract the active ingredients from tough types of ingredients, such as bark and roots, which are difficult to infuse. Decoctions can be made at home by simmering the plant material at just below boiling point for 6-8 hours, straining, squeezing and storing in the fridge for up to three days (see also Tincture). Decoctions may also be bought readymade from herbal suppliers.

Demulcent

This is a term given to plant extracts that have naturally soothing effects on the surface of the skin.

Diuretic

This is a substance that increases the flow of urine and reduces puffiness due to fluid retention.

Essential Oils

Essential oils are the fragrant, volatile and highly concentrated essences extracted from leaves, flowers, roots and bark of plants. The term 'essential' refers to the fact that they are essences.

Extract

This is a substance made by placing pieces of a plant or herb in water, alcohol or a solvent in order to remove its active ingredients. Once these have been removed, the liquid may be evaporated off, leaving behind the pure extract.

Free Radicals

Free radicals are the principal cause of skin ageing and most degenerative diseases. Damage is caused when highly active and destructive chemical compounds from oxygen are produced by oxidation. Processes that trigger the production of free radicals include ultra-violet radiation from the sun and airborne chemical pollutants.

Homoeopathy

Homoeopathy is a form of holistic medicine which is both safe and effective in treating numerous medical conditions. Based on the idea of helping the body to heal itself by providing traces of potentially toxic substances that trigger the body's own immune response.

Infusion

This is a preparation made by steeping a plant or herb in water to extract its active ingredients. An infusion is made by pouring boiling water over finely chopped plant material, such as leaves or dried flowers. Herb teas are simply an infusion of dried flowers, leaves, etc. Most parts of the plant are suitable for creating infusions, including ground stalks and powdered roots (see also Decoction). The infusion should be made by pouring boiling water on to the plant material and leaving to soak for up to 1 hour. Liquids should then be refrigerated and will last several days.

Inhalations

Many of the active ingredients in substances such as essential oils are carried through their smell. One way to make use of these is with an inhalation which carries the volatile components of the oil into the brain cells located at the top of the nose. The smelliest herbs with the highest volatile oil content are the most suitable for inhalations, e.g. thyme, rosemary, lavender, eucalyptus.

Lymphatic System

The lymphatic consists of a network of vessels or lymph channels that parallels the blood circulatory system. Lymph itself is a milky fluid that circulates around the body picking up debris and unwanted toxins from cells. Unlike the blood supply, the lymphatic system does not have the heart to pump it around the body and so relies on massage and exercise to keep it moving.

Medical Herbalism

Herbalism is a traditional form of medicine practised by those who have undergone lengthy professional training, and is recognised by the Medicines Act of 1968. Practitioners treat the patient as a whole and use herbal remedies to cure the long-term cause of the problem, not only its individual symptoms. The minimum length of training is four years, although many medical herbalists train for longer, and also study other healing arts such as acupuncture and iridology.

Mucilages

These are substances containing complex carbohydrates that give some plants a slimy quality. They are used in cosmetic preparations to make natural gels or to thicken liquids and creams e.g. carrageen moss. They are not absorbed by the body and pass through the system if swallowed, making useful bulking agents and laxatives e.g. linseeds.

Resins

Resins are gummy secretions from tree bark that melt when heated. They are mostly insoluble in water so need to be used in an alcohol solution. Resins contain many powerful healing agents and are highly antiseptic e.g. Balm of Gilead and myrrh.

Tannins

Tannins are substances found in plant leaves and bark containing natural phenols. They have astringent qualities and are useful in skincare to tone and protect the skin.

Tincture

Similar to a decoction or an infusion, a tincture is made by steeping the plant in a mixture of alcohol and water. Tinctures are especially suitable for plants that have a high content of resins or essential oils. Because of their alcohol content, tinctures have a longer shelf-life and are more readily available in a highly concentrated form. Most herbal tinctures contain approximately thirty-five per cent alcohol.

Tonic

A tonic is any substance that promotes energy and well-being. In skincare the term is used for liquids that tone the skin and encourage an increased blood supply to surface skin tissues. Herbalists also use plant extracts as internal tonics to pep up the system and strengthen the skin from within. Most plant-based skincare recipes have a tonic effect on the skin.

INDEX

BY THE SAME AUTHOR

Vital Oils *(Vermilion)*

Save Your Skin with Vital Oils *(Vermilion)*

Eat Yourself Beautiful *(BBC Publications)*

Liz Earle's ACE Plan *(Boxtree)*

Weight Loss For Life *(Boxtree)*

Liz Earle's Bikini Diet *(Boxtree)*

Liz Earle's Lifestyle Guide *(Boxtree)*

Liz Earle's Quick Guides to *(Boxtree):*

Acne

Antioxidants

Aromatherapy

Beating Cellulite

Beating PMS

Cod Liver Oil

Detox

Dry Skin & Eczema

Evening Primrose Oil

Food Allergies

Food Combining

Food Facts

Hair Loss

Healthy Menopause

Healthy Pregnancy

Herbs for Health

Juicing

Post Natal Health

Successful Slimming

Vitamins & Minerals

Youthful Skin